How To Learn

Study Skills for Level 2
(GCSE, National Diploma)

including the effective use of English,
applying for jobs and further courses

Paul Eustice

ISBN: 978-0-9926088-9-7   Justifiedtext.co.uk   1st March 2015

CONTENTS

Introduction

Who and what is this book for?

This is for students on level 2 courses, which means GCSE, National Diploma or their equivalent. Your ages and backgrounds will vary widely but I am assuming you have in common, that you take the idea of learning seriously and want to know how to do it efficiently.

First, note that this book is designed to help you enjoy your time as a student. Not to *worry* about it, but to get control of the situation, take charge, and find out how to learning can be pleasurable. The more you like it the better you will be at doing it and vice versa.

It is not just a matter of learning a few tricks or techniques. What we need to do is to ask questions about how you manage the process. How does your mind work and what habits do you have that might help or hinder your learning? This is not about magic tricks, it is about YOU.

The general principles of studying

This is general advice about how to cope with your work. It includes

time management

place management

self management

time management

How much time does it take to do the work? How can you plan your time so you use it wisely? This next step may sound very obvious but bear with me ...

 1) make a **timetable** of the week. Include all seven days and all 24 hours.

Everyone's ideal structure or pattern will probably be different	Morning - what time does it start for you?	Afternoon	Evening - what time should it finish for you?
Monday			
Tuesday			
Wednesday			
Thursday			
Friday			
Saturday			
Sunday			

Enter what you are usually doing in those times. How many hours are left for work? How many are wasted and could be used for work? What does 'wasted' mean? We all need some social life and a rest. You have to get enough sleep (see the next heading). But do you need that much television or social media time? What about the times when you can't remember what you did, because it was probably nothing much? It if wasn't important enough to remember, perhaps you ought to be working at that time instead? The more limited your time is, the more important it is to make a fixed time for studying and keep to it.

2) Think about the **rhythm** of your life. Are you an early riser or a night owl? When do you work best? How can you best fit the coursework, working for money and relaxing / socialising time into a single week?

Biology rules, and nature has decided that most teenagers need just over 9 hours of good sleep every night. Patterns vary. Some people can't get to sleep before 11 p.m. and some can't stay awake that long. Some nights you have to stay up late because it's party time, and make up for it later. But in general terms, you need to find a regular pattern that is right for you and get enough sleep of the right kind  (undisturbed, not exhausted) at the right time. Each person's ideal routine might be different.

How many breaks do you need to work at your best? Too few are as bad as too many. If you are honest, what works best for you?

3) You need to be **goal-focused**. You can easily spend hours doing something that wasn't really necessary. Then you find you haven't done what carries most marks or makes the most difference.

You need to be sure what exactly you are supposed to be doing and why. What would good work look like? What makes a good result? **Do that**, not something else. If you are not sure, ask. And do it early on, before you waste time and effort.

4) Don't be caught out by **deadlines** or tests. Make a plan of the year. Show when tests and exams take place, and when projects are due in. Don't wake up one morning and find you have a deadline you can't meet. Plan now and start early. If something is due in on 5th, maybe you should give yourself the deadline of 1st, to really make sure it gets done on time?

Some people find long assignments frightening. When they lay out the work to be done and look at it in one large plan, they find it worries them and then can't work at all. Overcome that by breaking all work down into **smaller targets**. Do one piece at a time, feel a sense of achievement, and then move on.

Making a list of things to do is often useful, so long as you don't make two common mistakes:

- make the list so long it worries you and makes things worse

- think that making the list is the actual job, not just preparation for the real work

Make a list of immediate priorities. Put them in order of importance. Start at once on what is at the top of the list. Revise the list regularly to cross off what is done and make you feel better. As you get better organised, add things to the bottom which are due in later on – push the advance planning further into the future.

place management

What is the best place for you to work? Should it be:

quiet

well-lit

with fresh air

well organised

free from distractions?

Or do you work best with music playing? Are you working on a joint project that needs talking through?

Do you need to keep an eye on young children at the same time? You may have to fight for space and time against others who need the room or your attention.

Do you need a workshop with tools, or a computer?

Whatever the case, you need to know, perhaps by experiment, how you work best. Then you need to work in that way as often as possible.

If you can, find the ideal place and stick to it. If you can't, perhaps you should be using the library? Leave home earlier, or leave college later, to make use of the facilities. Arrive early and then have a canteen breakfast to reward your labours.

Could you use your local library Saturday morning?

♫ ♫ ♫

If you do need music, think about what kind. A rhythm of 60 beats per minute actually helps you learn. Most modern music has a rhythm of 100 - 140 beats per minute. That lowers your brain's ability to keep hold of information. Why not try a different beat?

self-management

What kind of person are you? You need to know your own **strengths and weaknesses** so you can take control of your own future. You need to set **targets** for yourself so you are in charge of your own life.

Confidence is important. It is quite common to think everyone else is more confident than you are. Often, other people feel just as nervous, but they are hiding it and wondering if you noticed. But you can't let being nervous about work stop you from getting started on it. If you suspect you are just too scared to get started, write anything just to put some words on the paper. Get started, get into it, do better and then rip up the stuff you started with.

What you **eat** affects your work. It also matters **when** and **how** you eat. You should always eat breakfast. This gives you energy you will need to cope with the work. In general, all meals should have the kind of food that releases its energy slowly. Sugary foods give you a quick rush but they leave you tired again too quickly. Sugary foods can make you feel worse in the long run. Most people need more water and less sugar. Section 5 will give you more detailed advice and explain how it all works.

You need to be organised, and keep control of notes and reading lists from day one, but the way you do it may be unique to you. Decide on your strengths and work to them while you try to improve any weaknesses. You may find it useful to team up with somebody who has a quite different style, who is the opposite, so you can help each other out.

Some places offer mentors and some people benefit from learning support. If you think either would be useful then make sure you apply a.s.a.p. If you are studying on your own, you can look at **on-line support systems.** Some are factual - *www.howstuffworks.com* and some are subject-based -

http://www.bbc.co.uk/education/levels/z98jmp3.

But don't spend so much time on-line reading about studying that you don't actually do any. Think about your work, then get stuck in and do some.   The key is to know who you are. Know why it matters in your life as a student. Do something about it.

Time is easily wasted. Not making progress makes you less confident. It is then a vicious circle.

Break out by being organised so you can make your use of time more efficiently. This will increase confidence.

If you find something difficult, ask for help at an early stage.

Self-analysis

The scale below is 1-5.

You score 5 for a major strength – something you are good at which will help you through the course.

You score 1 for a major problem – something you are not good at which may hold you back.

Score 3 if you are about average or neutral. 3 is OK but not particularly impressive. You are aware of it but not worried about it.

number	Statement	score
1	I have thought about how I learn. I know how my own mind works and how to get the best out of it.	
2	Studying comes naturally to me. It may be hard work but I think I know how to do it.	
3	I have a place I can use for learning. I organised it for that purpose and it suits me well.	
4	I am always on time for classes and meetings. (On time means if it starts at 9.a.m. you are ready to start at 9 a.m.)	
5	I always meet deadlines.	
6	I find it easy to make notes when I am in class.	
7	I find it easy to make notes when I am	

	reading.	
8	I can usually find out the information I need.	
9	If I am given a long text, I can usually find what I want in it. I get to the right information quickly.	
10	I can sort through a lot of information quickly.	
11	I can find information in my notes even weeks after I have made them.	
12	When I read my notes weeks later they make sense.	
13	I plan longer projects well. I get the right information on time. I know how to organise information so I don't drown in it.	
14	I can write essays. I know how to organise them.	
15	I can take part in discussions without being too nervous or upsetting anyone else.	
16	I can make a presentation to my group without feeling too nervous. I get my point across clearly.	
17	I can study what I find interesting, but can't easily get down to anything else	
18	When a job needs doing, I organise and get started on it in good time.	
19	I enjoy taking exams	

20	I always know how to revise the right thing in the right way	
21	I may be a little nervous sometimes, but stress never stops me working or doing my best	
22	In a room full of people, I can concentrate. They do not distract me.	
23	I can work well with other people on joint projects.	
24	If I need to write something, I know how to get started and organise the information on the page.	
25	I don't have any problems with punctuation, grammar or spelling, so my written work does not suffer from technical errors.	
26	When it is time to move on, I can apply for a course or job with confidence	

When you have responded to the statements, go through them looking for any that you graded 5. These need urgent action. It may be a long term aim but it has to start today.

What kind of problem is this? What kind of answer does it need? Do any of the other study skills sections in here provide answers? Is there anyone you can talk to about it (other students, friends, teachers, mentors, counsellors, on-line communities)? What kind of practical steps can be taken to improve matters?

Targets need to be SMART:

specific - they say exactly what has to be achieved

measurable – so you can prove they have achieved them

achievable – they can be achieved in a realistic time frame

realistic - they are within the limits of your potential

time-related - they have deadlines you really can keep

Don't try to become perfect overnight – it just gets depressing when you fail. If you have to improve something, can you break them down in stages? For example, if you are notoriously bad at timekeeping and deadlines, try to be less late every day by an agreed amount and give yourself false deadlines that get earlier for each project.

When you have done something about all the level 1s start on your 2s, one at a time. You can always adjust your scores as you make progress (or realise you had been a shade too generous with yourself at the start).

To find out exactly how to make progress, just keep going

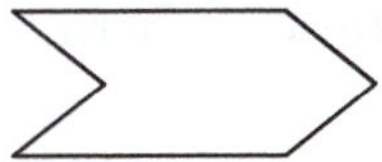

Learning Styles - do they really help?

According to popular theory, different kinds of people learn in different ways. They have different ways of thinking. They approach questions from different angles. They handle information in different ways. They have a different **learning style**.

Your learning style has nothing to do with intelligence, ability or experience of the subject. It is claimed that once you understand what your learning style is, you can play to your strengths and it gets much easier to learn.

This is only a theory and some versions of it are not to be taken too seriously, as they try to put everyone into complicated categories without enough proof to back it up. But the simple versions included below contain enough common sense elements to help you think about how you learn, so they are worth looking at briefly as a kind of shorthand to understand how your own mind works. Then we can move on.

The models

There are a number of models we can use to gain a better understanding or your own thinking, to learn more effectively. One is the VAK model - visual, auditory or kinaesthetic – and the other is right brain/left brain.

Putting it simply:

Visual - learn through seeing. They like to see pictures and diagrams. They like demonstrations, reading or videos.

<table>
<tr>
<td></td>
<td>Auditory - learn through hearing. They like to listen to tapes, lectures, debates, discussions and verbal instructions.</td>
</tr>
<tr>
<td></td>
<td>Kinaesthetic - learn through physical activities and direct involvement. They like to be hands-on, moving, touching and experiencing. Ideally, you would use all equally well</td>
</tr>
</table>

Many people have a tendency to use one more than the others, often without realising it.

In addition to this, the different sides of your brain are said to have different ways of working. Some people prefer to use the left side more than the right aside, others vice-versa.

 The **left side of your brain** specialises in academic aspects of learning – language and mathematical processes, logical thoughts, sequences and analysis. Left-brained people prefer a slow step-by-step build up of information. They like logical, step-by-step process, rules and order.

The **right side of your brain** is mainly concerned with creative activities. It uses rhythm, music, visual impressions, colour and pictures. Right brain people need to see the big picture, to have an overview. They can leap quickly from one thought process to another, which can be both creative but also confusing. Like being right or left handed, you might have a strong tendency to use one side more than the other, but without knowing it 

Does your brain think those images and text are the wrong way round? Some will and some won't - our brains work differently.

How does your brain work?

You could try and find out by using a questionnaire, but that has several disadvantages:

To be accurate, a questionnaire often has to be long and complex. If it is easy to fill in then it probably gives you a very crude version of how your mind really works.

Subconsciously, people often try to guess the 'right' answers, perhaps the answers that give the best impression or might give the most flattering result, so it give an inaccurate picture.

In any case, your learning style 'preference' is not some kind of permanent label. It is not what you are forever, just an idea of how your mind works at this stage of development. The key to success is active self-awareness, so you can look at your own mind and help it along. Keep an eye on it and see how it is working and perhaps even changing.

To do that you don't need to keep taking questionnaires but to ask yourself a simple question – "what makes life easier for me?" Effective learners look carefully at their own preferences and then work out ways of playing to their strengths. Only you can work out what is best for you in any context and at any stage of development.

Bearing this in mind, you can now look in more detail at descriptions of each kind of learner. Think about statements that might describe your strengths or limitations. Where do you recognise yourself and when do you feel obviously different to the people described?

As you work through them, don't look for a label to hang round your neck or a badge to wear. Look for ideas about how your mind works that might help you to understand yourself. You may be a complicated mixture of tendencies. You may find no simple label explains which style you prefer or dislike most. What matters is not what you are called but what you can learn about the best way to receive and manage information.

The way you explore the ideas may be a clue to what kind of learner you are. Will you read through it word by word on your own or discuss it with others? Will you use the diagrams and pictures to help make things more clear? Would it help to cut the text into sections and move them round on the desk, re-arranging them for yourself? Do what comes naturally. Note how you deal with the ideas as you work through them.

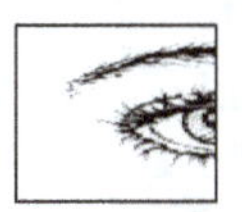 **Visual Learners** take in new information through pictures, diagrams, charts or films. They learn best by visualising what they are learning, creating pictures or diagrams. They like to see things written down for them. They might rely on seeing the speaker's body language and facial expressions to help them understand the lesson.

They can be good spellers and have good handwriting. They like to doodle in class. They like to be given an overview of the subject before they get stuck in to it.

They tend to notice what there is to be seen around them, so if they work in a messy place, or somewhere with too much to look at, they will find it hard to concentrate.

If you are a visual learner, then to help you learn better, you should:

- **always write down key facts** – try using flashcards – and look at it often

- try to use **diagrams and colour coding,** or making a picture of key ideas.

- plan your work by using **mind maps, spider diagrams and**

    flowcharts

- keep your **desk tidy** and when you get copies of **material file it straight away.**

Auditory learners prefer the spoken word; they use the speaker's tone of voice and other elements of speech (speed and pitch) to interpret the underlying meaning.

They prefer being given step-by-step instructions for learning tasks. They can discuss and argue well but are easily distracted by noises and other people talking.

If you are an auditory learner, then:

- try **reading aloud** to yourself

- **make tapes** to play in the car or personal stereo

- **explain your subject to someone else** (perhaps another auditory learner). A good way to get ideas organised is to hear yourself trying to explain them. Once you are clear, a good way to remember them is to keep telling them to other people.

- **ask questions** to make sure you've understood correctly.

- after you have read something, **summarise it and read it aloud to yourself**

 **Kinaesthetic or practical learners** learn through moving, doing and touching. They enjoy "hands on" activities, getting physically involved. They like to make something and handle objects.

They might be talking to themselves internally when learning. They like demonstrations and making models. They can find it difficult to sit still for long periods of time and concentrate. They are easily distracted and when concentrating will fidget. They might feel the need to walk around as they read or learn.

They like internet or virtual reality. They enjoy role play and prefer to make progress through trial and error. They need to do things to remember them.

If that is your type, you should:

- **practise** what you're learning as much as possible

- if you can't do it physically then put **key points on post-its**, and move them around from time to time as you read them

- **trace words** as you are saying them

- learn facts by **writing them out several times**. Make study sheets

- If you feel restless, **get something you can handle, squeeze or fidget with in** class without distracting others - a squeezy ball or worry beads.

Left brain learners

You prefer to learn in sequence, doing things logically step by step.

You like to be organised in your approach, to break things down into categories and to consider these separately.

You are good at thinking in terms of cause and effect. You like to do one thing at a time. You like attending to detail. You like rules and structure.

You work from small steps up to the big picture. You would learn best through words, lists, ordering things logically.

Right brain learners

You can use lateral thinking. You are flexible, and like to use your imagination and be creative, but those with a very strong right brain preference may also be disorganised. You can be impatient of rules, structures and details.

You enjoy creative activities, with rhythm, music, visual impressions, so might learn best through colour, shape, patterns and tunes.

Right-brain people need to see the big picture, to have an overview.

Dyslexic learners are often right brain (but that doesn't mean right brain people will be dyslexic).

Useful techniques for right-brain thinkers are:

- overviews - summaries, reviews, key points, etc.
- case studies, demonstrations
- models, systems, e.g. flow diagrams which describe the whole process in simple form
- mind maps, especially when used to summarise a topic

- pictures, images, graphs, charts, use of colour, shape, and patterns
- doing things physically, hands on: manipulating, moving etc.

You like to see things in the round, to consider the whole. You focus on similarities, patterns, and connections with what you already know. You like to get a 'feel' for the topic, and see how it all fits together. You prefer to follow your intuition rather than work things out carefully.

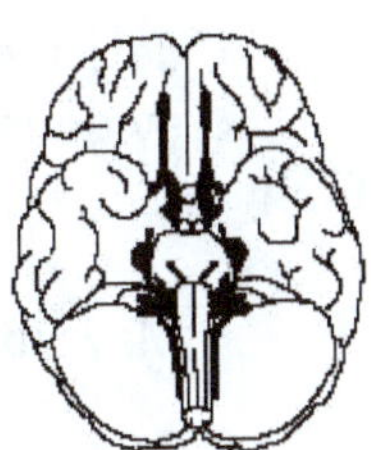

Ideally, you should be able to use both sides of your brain, and make sure you use whichever is most appropriate to the task at hand. If you are strongly left or right brain, you may wish to spend some time developing the weaker half by trying some of the techniques above.

Meanwhile, here is simple summary:

left brain

Likely advantages Could be good at :	**Possible disadvantages** May suffer from a tendency to:
remembering sequences,	accept problems instead of trying to overcome them;
logical planning,	

being ordered and organised.

repeat what you have been taught rather than think for yourself;

miss connections between topics;

learn skills in one area but fail to transfer them to another area.

May need to plan action first and may have trouble making decisions without clear evidence

right brain

Could be:

May suffer from:

flexible, creative and good at improvisation and problem solving;

poor logical planning and poor memory for sequences

good at seeing the wider picture and at making unusual connections;

poor organisation and time-keeping

willing to take risks and to join discussion.

Might find it hard to monitor your own learning and be unclear about boundaries.

Might have a good visual memory.

Now you have been through those ideas, does it help to explain what was hard or easy before? Can you see ways to apply them to your work in future?

The next section will explore different ways to record and manage information. There are lots of different ways to organise and record information. The way you record something you have just learned will be quite different from the way you record something you know quite well.

Choose an important part of your course. Get into small groups with others who share the same learning style. Experiment to see how many ways you can lay out that material for the people in your group.

Think about which ways suit your learning style. Experiment. Make life easier for yourself by doing what works best for you.

Remember - notes always need a title and date. Put your name on them in case they get lost.

Now we can turn to ways in which you can apply what you have just been thinking about.

Applying self-analysis as you record and store information

When you receive new information from someone else you have to understand it, record it, file it, revise it and then use it later to prove you have understood it.

When you are working out a process for yourself there are ways of laying it out that make it easier to think clearly and to handle the ideas even when they get complicated.

Consider the examples below.

Example One - a simple recipe for making bread at home.

It took a long time to write down because the person explaining it found it was easier to do it than to explain everything in the right order. It may take a long time to read.

1) weigh out the flour – 2 $\frac{1}{2}$ lbs of wholemeal and $\frac{1}{2}$ lb of strong white.

2) put it in a bowl in the oven on gas mark 2

3) when warm, mix in 2 packets of yeast

4) then mix in a tablespoon of salt. You can add a small handful of shelled sunflower seeds if you want to.

5) Make a well in the middle of the mixture and put into it half a tablespoon of soft brown sugar, two tablespoons of olive oil (or corn oil, or an ounce of butter), 1$\frac{1}{2}$ pints of water. Use a spoon to mix this together. As it becomes sticky, start to use your hands. Keep mixing until you have a smooth dough.

6) Turn it out on to a cool surface and knead it for ten minutes. This means bashing it and pushing it about to make it more elastic and smooth.

7) Put it in a large bowl and cover it loosely with greased clingfilm. You want to exclude the air but allow for it to double in size.

8) Two hours later, take it out and gently knead for a few minutes to remove all the air again.

9) Cut it into three even pieces and place it in to buttered loaf tins.

10) Leave it for 30 minutes. Meanwhile, preheat the oven to gas mark 5.

11) Place on the middle shelf for 35 minutes.

12) Turn out the loaves and place then back in the oven upside down for a few minutes just to brown the base.

13) Tap the base – if it sounds hollow then the loaf is done.

14) Leave to cool on a wire tray.

Do you think that is the best way for you to take in that information?

If not, what would be better for you? If so, is that the best way to remember it?

Would it be better with pictures. If you can't draw it can you use photographs? Or are crude sketches good enough to remind you?

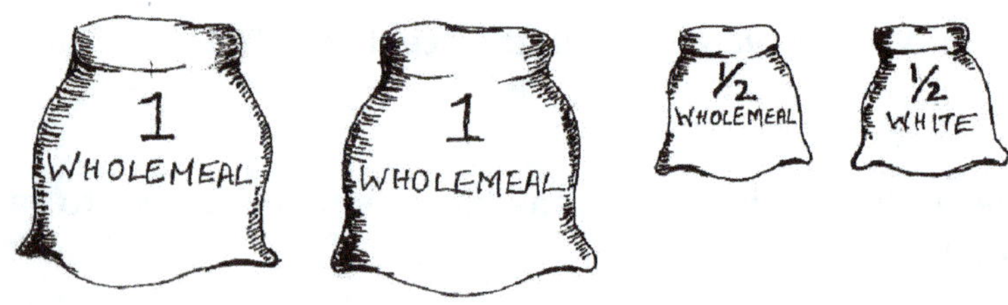

Would it help to use shorter sentences but put the words in big type and boxes like this?

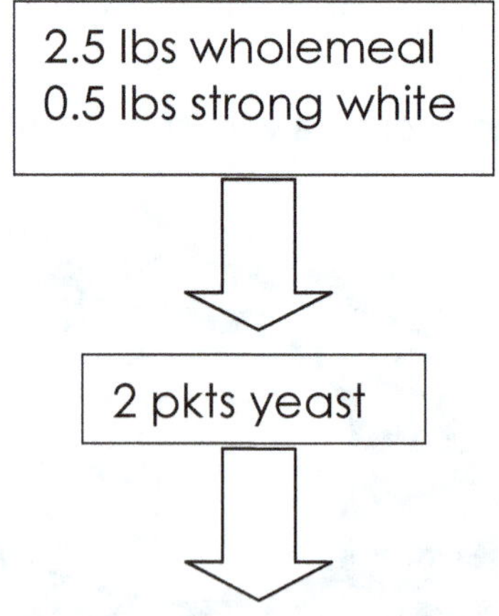

That sort of block system is useful for representing simple processes, such as food turning to energy:

You can put extra notes inside the boxes or beside the diagram (here) but keep them simple so you can take it all in at once and remember it as a kind of picture.

ingestion (swallow)

digestion

nutrition

energy

When you make notes you are taking in someone else's information and turning it into **your** information. It has to be in your own words and laid out in a way that suits you. This is an active process. You must make a conscious decision about how you learn, and adapt material to your own style. You need to be in control.

At first you may feel you need to write down a lot of detail. You may find you can't remember very much and you are not sure what will be important. Later, as you learn more about the subject, you get to know what matters and what doesn't. You learn to prioritise and select. You grow more confident and can simplify your notes.

As you gain more experience, existing notes should be re-written in a simpler form. Apart from saving space and making it easier to find information, the process of rewriting notes in different formats will itself help you to understand the material, and fix it into your long-term memory.

Notes may be made when reading or when attending classes. The process is different. Why do you make them and how should you make them?

There are many different ways of taking notes depending on:

> The way your mind works
> The kind of information you are dealing with
> What you want to use the notes for
> The amount of time available to make them

And there are several different reasons for doing it:

> Focusing your attention - making notes stops your mind from wandering as you read or listen to someone speak.

> Making sense of information – the process of reading or listening becomes active and forces you to find some sense in the words.

> A sign of progress – good notes make you feel more secure. You feel you are taking control.

A form of external memory for later, when you need to produce reports or essays and have to refer back

You need to keep looking back at your notes asking yourself, "are they doing the job that I want?", "could I be using my time more effectively?" and changing your approach to get the best result.

In general, notes should:

a) record your **source.** For a book, you may need the title, page number and library reference.

b) show the **main ideas** clearly.

c) show the **relationship** between main points and supporting points – does point a prove point b or is it an example?

d) be **brief,** or you won't be encouraged to read them again. So they are wasted. Use abbreviations if you can to speed up the process. But make sure you will remember what they stand for later on.

e) be **selective.** Avoid material that is not relevant. If you are not sure, keep it for now but perhaps erase it later in edited versions.

f) be in **your own words**. You may need to use key words from the text but be clear about the difference between this and copying out large chunks. That is not really an active thinking process and does not help you to understand.

g) be **well spaced** so you can add to them later if necessary. Obviously, it is easier to change notes later on if they are word processed, but keep a back up copy just in case.

What most people tend to do, automatically, is to use **linear or serial notes** – words in lines on a page. If you are using them to record someone speaking, or the main points of what you are reading, then don't write too much. Select the most important points. Concentrate only on words or phrases that will help you recall the content, and add to them later if necessary. But don't leave it there. If you read it again in an hour, does it still make sense? In two days? How long before you forget what the short notes were supposed to mean? How much would you need to add later to explain it to yourself in your own words, and how quickly would you need to expand?

For the first version, try to use headings, sub-headings, numbered points, bullets – anything to build in order and logic. You might write the main headings on the left of the page with subheadings and examples indented:

<u>Heading</u>

subheading 1

 information and examples

xxxxxxxxxxxxxxxxxxxxxxxx

 xxxxxxxxxxxxxxx

 xxxxxxxxxxxx

subheading 2

subheading 3

Notes do not need 'proper sentences'. Cut down space by using only the essential words. You might use your own abbreviations as a kind of shorthand – Pgt for Piaget or dl for diesel. But don't forget what they stood for. You may need a key written down somehere.

Leave a wide margin (for additions and cross-referencing) and leave plenty of space around notes for additions and alterations.

Other layout options include:

> Record the page number of books in the extreme left margin for quick reference.

> Write on one side of the paper only - so that the left hand page in your file is blank for additions - or a pattern note.

> Underline, highlight and mark creatively to aid memory of key points.

> **Diagrams and tables are often underused. Don't just look for them in books or online - make your own,. Being active and making your own makes the information stick in your mind.**

Once you have collected information, it is sometimes useful to place them in a table to organise and compare. For example:

Note Making Method	Best for	Main Advantages	Possible Disadvantages
Linear	Information that comes to you already in order – stories, methods, lists etc. Right brainers?	Records detail and probably in phrases that might be used later for representing	Can be overwhelming in detail; key ideas may get lost in superfluous detail; slavishly follows other people's order and logic.
Mind maps /spidergrams	Brainstorming, organising connections. Visual learners and left brainers?	Quick, flexible, reflects the way a mind actually works.	Not everyone finds it sympathetic; can be messy and often need linear notes to complete organisation.

You can use blocking and chart layouts for various kinds of information. It is useful for sorting out basic facts. Is it easier to take in and recall this way than it might be laid out as ordinary sentences?

Flow charts

If you are trying to note down a process, then flow charts can organise ideas clearly. This might be a simple technical process or a decision-making process (algorithm)

You may have software that does it for you – some can be downloaded for free and the Word 'Draw' toolbar offer a flowchart option. But a pencil sketch is good enough to clarify the ideas in your mind. It is not worth spending hours on making pretty charts with the computer if, when it is over, you have only increased your own understanding very slightly . Put the effort where it really pays off – focus on the main task.

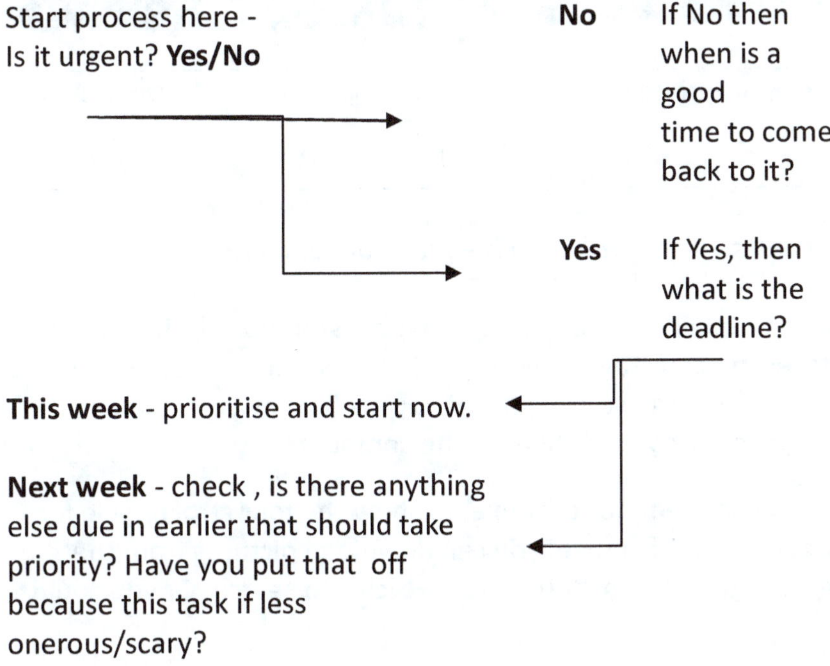

(you can make this in Word using tables and or / insert text box and insert shapes, choosing the arrow shape) - or just use a pencil!

Here are some more ways to record and display information:

Storyboards are used when making films. They help the director plan, to know what pictures to shoot next and what lines of script go with them. They can also be used to show stages in a technical process -

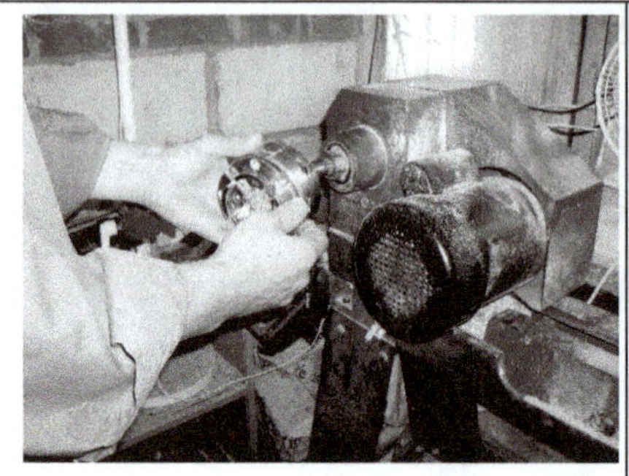	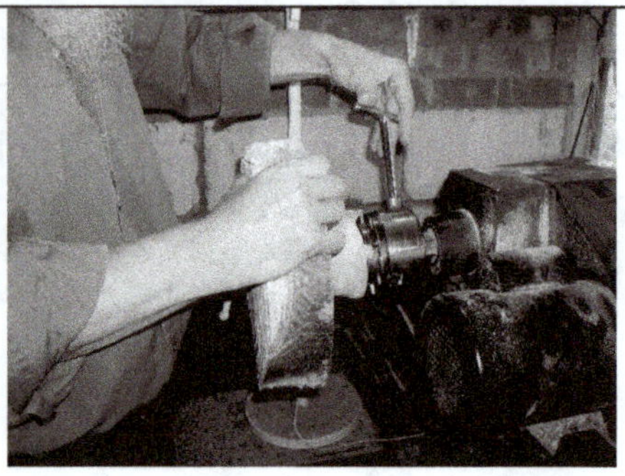
Place appropriate chuck on the spindle	Clamp wood securely inside chuck

You can use 'insert table' to keep it all under control

You can explain simple processes with a storyboard, showing pictures of each stage as you bleed brakes, set up a lathe, create a pavlova or set the stage lights. If you can't draw you can take photographs and load them to the computer.

You can use them, for example, to show the four stroke cycle for a petrol engine. Of course, you can download pictures from the internet. Just type in "four+stroke+cycle" to search. Or you could try:

http://techni.tachemie.uni-leipzig.de/otto/otto_g0_eng.html
http://www.illawarra.net.au/transport/fourstrk.htm
http://www.howstuffworks.com/engine.htm/printable

The last one is even animated, but be careful. Printing pictures from the screen and filing them in your notes doesn't in itself help you learn anything. If you draw your own as well, the process of

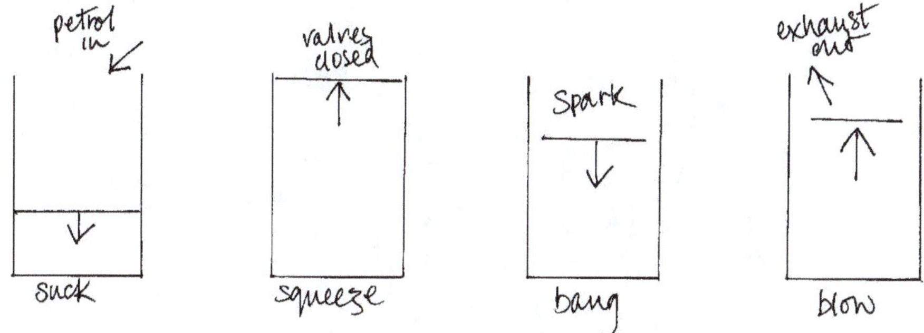

using your hands and eyes together as you make the pictures will help the ideas to stick in your memory. You might download a coloured picture which is impressive but complicated. For learning purposes, you might then turn it into a sketch like this: Making your own sketch, however rough, is more use in understanding a process than downloading someone else's. When your eye, hand and brain work together, you are making it easier to learn.

Mind maps, sometimes called spidergrams. are useful for organising ideas in two ways.

To brainstorm. If you have a question to answer you write down whatever comes into your head, using boxes and arrows to make connections then sorting it out afterwards. The first version might be messy but gets something on paper quickly:

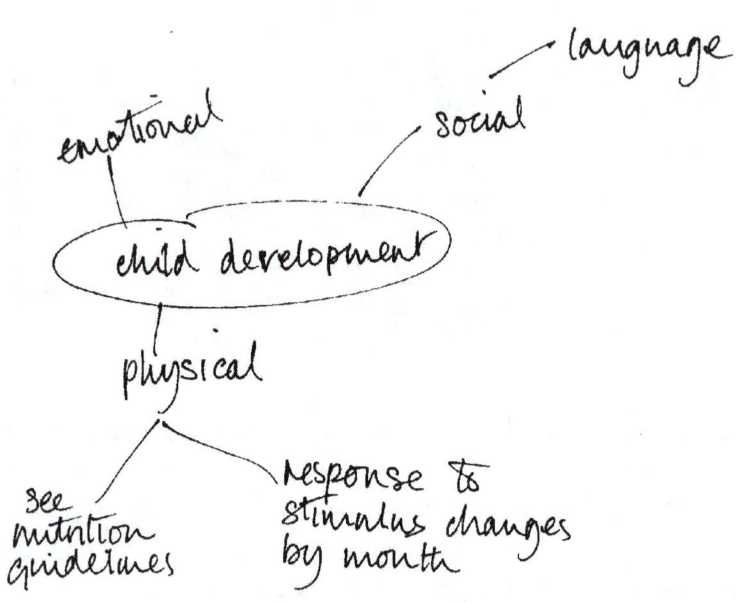

Then you can start to organise it better for filing or sharing:

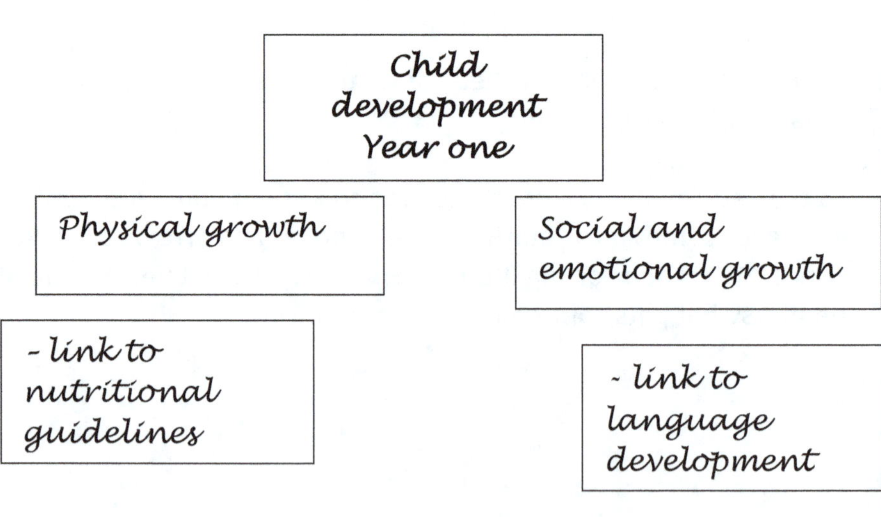

You could then start to make a finished poster, or a chart of connected ideas:

Age	Motor skills	Emotional	Social	Language skills
First mont h		Generalised tension	Helpless	
2-3 mont hs	Controls eyes muscles and lifts head	Smiles at face, can be upset or happy	Can be soothed by rocking	
4-6 mont hs		Responds to tone of voice and own name without visual clues	Recognis es faces.	Responds to tone of voice and own name without visual clues

Advantages of mind maps include:

Notes are on one page. You have to be brief. They are good for revising because you can see the main ideas quickly in one place.

You can make your notes in outline, with the main points first, and then go back and add details later without rewriting.

Points are grouped together.

They force you to organise the information so you can see at once the main topics and links between ideas..

One sheet of paper looks much easier to deal with than pages of ordinary notes.

But problems may include:

Not everyone has a mind that works visually. Some people find it confusing.

A map that reflects closely the way your mind works may not make much sense to anyone else

For that reason, and for producing essays, reports and presentations, you have to turn the map into linear notes later.

Rhymes and mnemonics

If you prefer an aural system, try to record notes on tape and listen to them on your earphones as you travel in. You might find certain musical clues as a backing that go with main points and act as a kind of mnemonic. Mnemonics use the initial letters of a list to make a memorable word or sentence. An example in Wikipedia helps you remember the names of the plants:

Mercury, **V**enus, **E**arth, **M**ars, **J**upiter, **S**aturn, **U**ranus, **N**eptune

becomes

My **V**olkswagen **E**mits **M**ick **J**agger **S**ongs **U**ntil **N**oon

which is much sillier so more likely to stick in your memory.

If you can't recall what order to pot the balls in a game of snooker, you could recite "**you go brown before potting black**" **to remember the order yellow, green, brown, blue, pink, black.**

If you can't remember which way to move a thread – clockwise or anti-clockwise, you could try "right = tight, left = loose".

Making notes during classes.

It will help if you know what is likely to happen. You could ask the teacher to offer you some headings before you start, or suggest them as you go along.

If you are using a blank page, always leave wide margins so you can go back later and add more detail or point up a connection.

Always review the notes as soon as possible afterwards, perhaps comparing your versions with others, and expect to edit them into a different format or at least tidy them into a more logical order so they will mean something weeks afterwards, when you may have forgotten every word that was said.

So, given what you know about yourself, your preferences, strengths and weaknesses and your subject, how should you record information?

Before you finish today, make sure you complete the action plan below.

Don't just rush it to get it finished. It affects your future. Think of it as the key to your future achievement.

Personal Record

My strengths are	My biggest weaknesses are	What I can do about it is

The first thing I am going to do is ....

I will do this (when/where?) ....

Eating and Learning

Learning is easier if your brain is working properly. Your brain is part of your physical body and works by chemical reactions. The wrong diet can make you tired, confused or aggressive.

The brain is only about 2% of our body weight but uses 20% of the energy available to the whole body, so any loss of energy affects the brain most.

We make energy from food. Your brain needs the right nutrients, carried in the blood stream when you digest food. What you eat affects how you feel and how you think.

The problem may be too much of the wrong food, like additives and sugar, or not enough of the right kind.

The chemicals that most upset the brain are often addictive, and a high sugar intake is one of the most common. The World Health Organisation (WHO) recommends that we should take no more than 10% of our calories as sugar, but some breakfast cereals are 40% sugar and doughnuts contain even more. Sugary drinks are a a major problem. Too much sugar reduces your ability to learn.

If you take in too much sugar at once, it can give you a rush of energy in the short term. Then the body defends itself from the excess by releasing more insulin to break it down quickly. Your blood-sugar level drop as dramatically as it rose. Then you feel tired again, so you feel you need more sugar.

If you eat the right food, it releases its energy slowly and keeps you balanced through the day. Porridge is a better start to the day that coke and doughnuts, but a good fry up may be justified if you are about to take a long test.

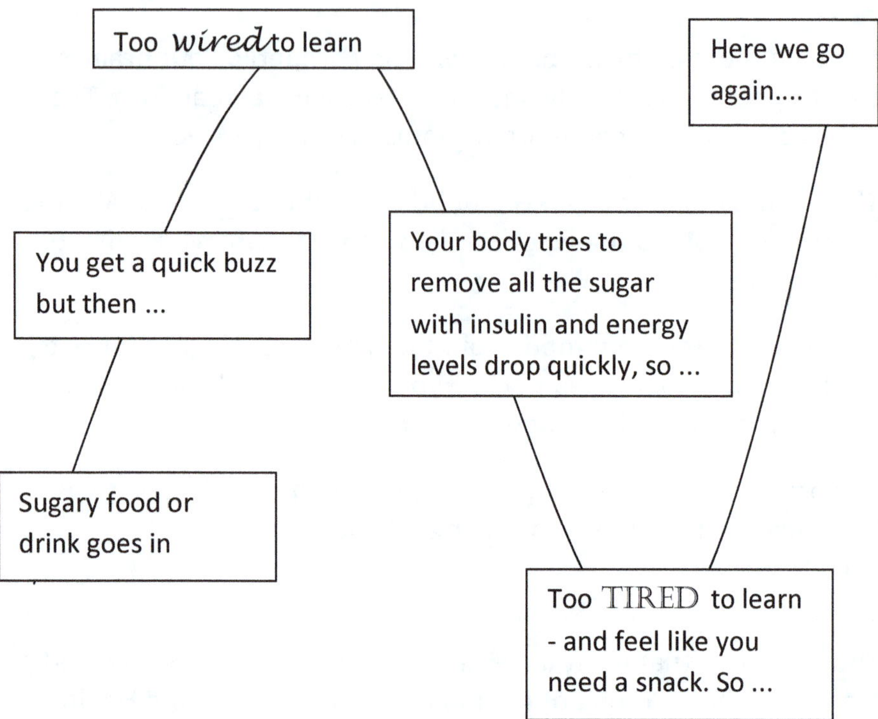

Eating properly doesn't mean we always have to eat stodgy and unexciting food. Good quality chocolate also provides useful minerals. It is a matter of getting the right kind of balance. A varied diet of slow-release foods will give you most energy when you most need it and avoids clogging the mental process.

The average adult eats roughly 13 grams (2 teaspoons) of salt a day. We only need about 3 -6 grams ($^1/_2$ – 1 teaspoon). Most of that salt is added during manufacturing. Excess salt leads to high blood pressure, so eating less processed, canned of packaged food would reduce it.

The body is between 50-70% water. If we don't take in enough fresh water we will not operate efficiently. A regular supply though the day – up to eight glasses - helps the brain to work better. Flavoured drinks are more likely to contain sugar and e-numbers.

Questions so far

A teaspoon of salt would

   a) be half your daily requirement
   b) be a maximum figure for any adult
   c) help the medicine go down
   d) decrease blood pressure

If you drink water, you need

   a) at least 10 pints per day
   b) 6-8 glasses on average
   c) sugar and additives to make it healthier
   d) 3-4 glasses every 24 hours

If you don't know the answer, what kind of reading have you been engaged in? How quickly can you scan back and find the answer? See the next section (6) for advice on reading.

Eating properly to feed your brain is quite easy. You just need to keep to these simple rules:

Eat a wide **variety** of foods

Make them **fresh** whenever possible

Eat a good **breakfast**

Drink more **water**

Reduce **refined sugar**, **salt** and **additives**

- anything **refined** or **processed** will do you less good

Proteins are used to build and repair your body. You get them from fish, eggs, lean meat milk, cheese, nuts, seeds and beans. Only about 10% of your diet should be protein, although anyone who is still growing, pregnant or breastfeeding, may need more. Even body-builders should never take in more than 20%.

Carbohydrates are the main 'fuel' for the body. They give you energy and help digestion. They should make up between 55 t0 60%. The brain needs a constant supply of carbs, but that doesn't mean you have to eat all day. You need to eat the kinds of food that will **release their energy slowly through the day**.

G.I (slow foods)

The rate at which carbs release their energy is measured by something called the Glycemic Index or GI. This is sometimes spelled glycaemic and is a measure of how the blood sugar levels change after you eat any carbohydrate.

Foods with a high GI release their energy quickly.

Foods with a low GI release their energy slowly.

Low GI foods are rich in fibre and make you feel full. They take longer to digest so you feel full for longer. They include oats, lentils, nuts, beans, barley, citrus fruits (like oranges), whole wheat bread and most vegetables.

Medium GI foods include muesli, wholemeal pasta and brown bread, some fruits, basmati rice.

High GI foods include sugar, other white rice, sweets and chips.

It is not always easy to know what GI rating applies to specific foods. Bread, for example, might be high, medium of low depending on whether it is white or made with varying degrees of whole grain. The general rule is to look for more fibre and less sugar, more fresh food and less processed.

The more refined and processed a food is, the quicker it will release its sugars and the more tired and irritable you will be afterwards – wanting to take in more for another high spot, which then wears off again. You might get heavier but you won't get more concentration.

Vitamins and minerals

These are needed by your body in various combinations. Rather than worry about how much you need of each separate kind, it is easier and safer to eat a varied diet of fresh food in the knowledge that it will probably provide the right balance.

For example, vitamin A is good for the brain and nervous system but an overdose can be toxic, especially in pregnant women. Most young people have too little. They could increase their supply of oily fish, carrots and oranges without taking in too much

Zinc and copper are found in the part of the brain that plays a major role in memory and learning. This area helps to control emotional response and stress. If you take in too much zinc it reduces the effectiveness of copper and vice-versa. The safest approach is a varied diet, not trying to fine-tune one element at a time.

Briefly, you probably need more water - certainly a supply throughout the day if central heating is drying out the air, but tap water in a recycled bottle is cheaper than bottled water and just as good for you. You need less meat than you think but could have more vegetables and fruit instead. You need far less sugar and salt and fewer additives.

Resources to explore further

On diet and behaviour in general, especially effects on learning, read Dr. Alex Richardson, Senior Research Fellow at Mansfield College Oxford. Her recent book, *They are what you feed them,* has fairly simple science written for parents who want to feed children for healthy development.

She is also Director of the charity FAB (Food and Behaviour) Research, which is at *http://www.fabresearch.org/.* This site has information on the effects of fatty acids on learning and behaviour and on a range of learning difficulties that may be associated with diet. It has separate information routes for parents, teachers and educational professionals, so you can pick out the easier articles to read on any subject. Her book can be ordered from the site.

The BBC has lots of useful ideas: *http://www.bbc.co.uk/health/treatments/healthy_living/index.sht ml*   and so does the NHS: *http://www.nhs.uk/LiveWell/Goodfood/Pages/Goodfoodhome.as px*

Reading

Why are you reading?

Where and when are you reading?

How are you reading?

If you read the wrong way, up to half the information you read is forgotten again in 15 minutes. This advice may save you time and effort.

Why are you reading?

Different kinds of writing need different kinds of reading. You may be reading for different purposes. Think about how you might read these:

magazine	railway timetable
manual for a new camera	graffiti on a wall
textbook for your course	email or text from a friend

Some you would skim over lightly. Others you would study very closely, but only one part at a time, after you found the right place. Some information you act on. You tend to remember it because you use it. Some information somehow just sticks in your mind without your trying, but other ideas just won't stay there and keep slipping out. This section will help you find the right way to read material that is important to your course.

Where and when are you reading?

Where and when you read can be as important. If you are very busy, you may have to make the best of every available minute by using train or bus journeys, but ideally you should try to find a chair that is comfortable, but not so comfortable you drop off. Make sure you have good light that does not cast shadows or cause glare on shiny paper. Put the 'phone on silent/answer. Use music if it helps. Make sure you have paper and pens for making notes. Then stay there until you achieve something.

How do you know when you have really achieved something?

Every time you sit down to read, spend the first few minutes remembering what you read before. If you can remember it, that makes you feel confident and prepares you for the next stage. If you can't, you need to go back to it before you move on.

When you are nearly at the end of your reading time, especially if you are getting tired, stop taking in new information and start looking over what you already know. Sort out your notes and make sure you will be ready for the next session.

Take regular breaks. Move about if you can. Don't just use up time staring at paper – use your time wisely to get something out of it. To do that you need to **read actively,** and the next section tells you how.

How are you reading?

skim, scan, detailed and critical reading

pqrst system

sq3r system

eye wandering

reading on screen

skim, scan, detailed and critical reading

Reading might be:

skimming,

scanning

or

detailed.

Skimming is a very quick run over the surface to see if it is likely to be relevant. You might choose a book from the shelf, a chapter in a book or a section of that chapter by skim reading. You quickly skim the surface until you see a reason to slow down. It may help to find the right book or the right place if you refer to such things as titles

contents page

introduction

blurb on the back cover

subheadings

summaries at the end of chapters

The next stage is to **scan** the text more carefully. You look at subheadings and glance quickly at the rest so you tune in and get an idea of what you are about to read. You may start to see how the main ideas are connected. It's like getting a rough idea of the territory before you start to explore properly.

Once you know you are in the right place, and know what you are in for, then you can settle down to more **detailed reading**. You may have to slow down from time to time and even re-read some of it to make sure you really understood it. You need to be able to explain the ideas in your own words, so you know you have really understood them.

You might be making notes as you go. If you are, don't forget to note page references, title, author and library number so you can go back to the original quickly if you need to. If it came from the internet, bookmark it or record the URL.

 If you are not just taking in information, you may also need to move on to **critical reading**. At this stage you can start to argue with the author's opinion or criticise their style. You may need to start choosing quotations for that purpose.

pqrst system

This helps to improve understanding and your memory for key ideas and information. The method can be used on all kinds of material. It can be long or short – the principle is the same. The initials stand for five stages:

>preview

>question

>read

>self-recitation

>test

preview

You preview the whole text by skimming through to get an idea of major topics. You can read the main headings and look quickly at any diagrams or illustrations. Check to see if there is a summary or conclusion at the end of the chapter and read that more slowly.

question

Look carefully at any chapter titles, headings and sub-headings. Try to imagine them as a question. For example, if the heading is 'roofs' and subheadings include 'elements of construction', 'timber' and 'flat roofs' then you might have questions like 'What technical parts do all roofs have to have? What do timber roofs have that flat roofs don't? What are flat roofs made of? What you are doing here is getting ready to ask the text questions, so it is speaking to you and offering answers. Instead of just staring at the page and hoping something happens, you are forcing the page to tell you something. You are reading actively, so you are more likely to stay awake and learn something.

If the text is long, and especially if it looks worrying, break it up and deal with it in bite size pieces. If there are subheadings, try to turn them into questions to be answered one at a time. If not, scan the text for a few pages to see what kind of question you could ask first.

read

Next, read the section carefully to try to answer those questions. You may find you have to change the question because, when you read carefully, you realise you jumped to the wrong conclusion. That is OK – the main thing is to make a real connection with the text. Make it talk to you and ask yourself if you understood it. Don't let it just run past your eyes without speaking to you. Make it stop and explain itself.

self-recitation

After you have finished reading, try to recall the main ideas and repeat the information. Put the ideas into your own words. Compare your version to the text and check you have translated accurately. Aural learners may wish to do this out loud, or even try to explain to another person as they take a break.

As you are doing this, the information will be fixing itself in your memory. If you have misunderstood anything, it will become clear to you as you try to explain and check.

test

When you have finished reading, you should test and review all of the material. Look over any notes you have made. Test yourself on the main ideas and then on the detail. If you feel confident you can move on. Later, you will recap all you learned this session before you start the next session, to make sure it stayed in place.

Another popular acronym is **SQ3R.** This stands for

survey

question

read

recite

review

That is just another way to offer the same advice, but the words have a better rhythm so it may be easier to remember.

The essence of the technique is to engage with the text, to approach it actively. Make your brain and the text work together until you feel in control and you know something is happening.

To see whether it helps, try to close your eyes and tell yourself the exact meaning of pqrst and sq3r. If you can't – and you have just read it – you ought to read it again, and this time apply it.

eye wandering

Most people assume that when we read our eyes move smoothly and evenly across the line of print. In fact, this is not so. Our eyes move in a series of stops and quick jumps.

Very slow readers only read one word at a time. Sometimes they skip back to words they have already read and allow their eyes to wander over other parts of the page.

It can help to go back over anything you haven't quite understood, but it should be deliberate and not just a wandering eye. If you find you are doing this more than you need to, try using a finger or a pencil to move across the lines and stop your eyes natural wander. Your eyes will move about less and you will feel less tired. Also, if you move the pen or finger smoothly and quickly your eyes will follow it and your reading will naturally speed up. Having a better rhythm will help you to understand the meaning of the passage in one go, instead of wandering off and getting lost so you have to start again.

All that will save you time and effort. Now wait for fifteen minutes and see if you can remember what this section was about, and explain it to someone else. If not, read it again and apply it as you go along.

Reading on screen (and tips for the disabled)

This can be bad for your eyes, so avoid glare and take regular breaks to rest them.

If you have a problem with reading or using a computer, you may be able to obtain help and equipment from Student Support. You may find the library (Learning Resource Centre) has some software, hardware or other support sytems already installed. Ask them.

If you are on your own, or at home, there are still several things you can do. For example, Windows has setting s under 'Accessibility' or 'Ease of Access' that will magnify the text and even read it to you.

web pages can be made much larger - press CTRL and + to make the whole page bigger (CTLR and - to reduce again).

 Or go to Tools - Internet Options - General and change the font or colour of any page. .

In **Word pages** you can change font and size in the usual way on the toolbar or use the zoom button to go from 100% to 500%. If you go to Format you can alter the background colour - a pale yellow is sometimes better for black print.

PDF means portable document format. Most people will read pdf files in Adobe Acrobat, which is usually fitted as standard. If not you can download it free. Foxit also have a free reader.[1]

PDF files can be read on or off line, but with certain differences.

If you read on line, you can use f11 to go 'full screen'.

You can also use the zoom tools (magnifying glass and + or - signs) to view the whole document in much larger print, or to magnify just a part of it for closer inspection.

---

[1] *http://www.foxitsoftware.com/Secure_PDF_Reader and http://get.adobe.com/uk/reader/ (untick the McAfee box first)*

If you download it to your own hard drive, you can also ask it to read the document to you even if you do not have your own screen reader. Go to the top tool bar and select View - Read Out Loud. Choose 'one page' or 'the whole document'. It will read to you over speakers or headphones. To pause or stop go back to view/read out loud.

The voice sounds like a robot but you can choose your reader - Sam. Michael or Michelle - by using Edit - Preferences. This also sets volume, speed and pitch.

Getting started - planning a piece of writing

A few minutes spent on planning can save a lot of wasted time later on. You may feel like plunging straight in and getting started, but walking quickly in the wrong direction is not making progress. On the other hand, sometimes the longer you put it off the worse it gets. Sometimes that blank piece of paper stares at you. The longer it is empty the worse it gets. The answer is to put something on it as soon as you can, but do it in a way that helps you plan later. Expect to have to change things later. Once you have one version, you may be able to improve it, but at least you feel better having something to work on.

1. Titles and subtitles

Some people like to work very logically to decide on the headings they will use first, then break them down into smaller units.

Title

Main heading 1

Subheading – key words or main points.

Subheading – key words or main points.

Subheading – key words or main points.

Main heading 2

2. Bubbles

At the other extreme, some people, or the same person with a different topic, may have no idea where they are going yet, and need to get something down on paper to get started at all. They need to do something about that blank paper that is staring at them and putting them off.

In that case, just fill the page with some circles and start to write an idea in each circle that might be useful. As one idea leads to another, add more circles then, when you have enough, lean back, look at the overall shape of the information, and start to number them in order.

3. Mind map

A mind map is one stage further. You can draw connections between the bubbles, and branch off to new ideas so that your plan goes off in several directions. Then you can rub out the ones you don't need, number the ones you do and even start to make headings and subheadings if you prefer.

4. Sticky notes or post-its (for kinaesthetic learners and fidgets)

If you find sitting in front a piece of paper off-putting, try using the whole room and moving about. Write each idea you have for the piece on a post-it then group ideas together to form a plan. If you have to move, you can take a photograph of your plan and load it into your computer later on.

5. Dictaphone (for aural learners and people who keep losing their files, or find lots of paper offputting.)

Or you can talk to yourself. Walk about, go shopping, walk through the woods, but take something with you that records ideas as you have them. Sometimes, when you give up trying to remember something or solve a problem, the answer then pops into your head from your subconscious. It may be better for you to stop trying, but be ready to record it when it happens. Then, once you get started, keep on recording the next idea until you have enough to listen to that you can write down and use.

Some opening gambits for essays

Sample title:
Explore the concepts of feminine or masculine.

The Obvious Distinction

A common error is to start by quoting the dictionary definition of a key term. This can look as if you have no ideas of your own and are slightly desperate. The opening sentence should arrest the reader's attention and give them the confidence that you have something to say. They can read the dictionary without your help, so you need to move on a stage further. What can be very useful to them is when you make some point they may not have thought of, to help clear up a potential confusion or common error.

> We may first distinguish between female and feminine, or between sex and gender. Sex is a function of biology but gender is only a social construct.

The Rhetorical Question

> Does the term 'feminine' describe qualities in the woman it is applied to or does it betray attitudes and values in the person using it?

It isn't strictly rhetorical, as you are about to answer it, but it allows you to set the terms of the debate from the very start, and gets you straight to a major point. It can lead to useful distinctions. If you are genuinely ambivalent, a question is a good place to start, so you can take both sides in turn. If you have a strong view you can ask a question then show why there can only ever be one sensible response to it.

The Strong (challenging) Opinion

> Women who describe themselves as feminine are often valuing themselves for those qualities of simpering weakness which demean them and keep them in the place men have designed for them.

or

> One of the natural consequences of women insisting on their own strength and equality is that New Men have come to value their own weakness and dependence, to the point that New Women find them just as disappointing as the Old Men, albeit for opposite reasons.

You can always qualify it later, but at least the reader knows you will keep them awake.

The Paradox

> What society seems to value and praise as feminine are qualities which, in practice, it punishes.

Now you've got them intrigued, you can explain.

The intriguing detail.

> My cousin is the most feminine person I have ever met, and his girlfriend is the most masculine.

There are many other ways to start, and what the good ones have in common is that they make the reader feel confident. They may or may not understand you straight away, but they feel they might and that you are worth the effort.

How to work on projects or reports

clarify your purpose

Read carefully and discuss exactly what you are supposed to be doing, and why.

What are you supposed to be proving with this work? What criteria will be used to judge it? Who will read it and what will they hope to gain from it? (NB most work has two kinds of audience – the people it pretends to be for and the person who grades it. Do not confuse them)

brainstorm and mind map

You can start by letting your mind run wild and thinking all kinds of wild ideas to get you started. The most crazy idea may turn out to be the most useful and really original. But once you have some useful ideas, make sure you use mind maps to organise them, and turn them into sub-headings. Make sure the sub-headings closely relate to your purpose in writing it.

 ## clarify your time frame

Make a note on a large poster and in your diary of the final date for handing it in. If at all possible, move back a week and aim for an earlier deadline to play safe. Work out roughly how long you think you can spend on each of the following stages, and keep track of your progress.

control information

Once you are clear what you need to produce, then decide what kind of information you will need to produce it. List possible sources (libraries, internet, friends, handouts and old notes from previous lessons)

Beware of three major problems:

1) Gathering so much you don't know what to do with it. As it comes in, start to keep ideas and information under separate headings, or in separate folders (e.g. with Word) so it has some kind of organisation from the very beginning. In fact, you may start by analysing the best headings, then seeking information to go under them, and maybe add and subtract headings as information comes in.

2) Forgetting where you found it, so you can quote a reference in your bibliography. Write it down at once and keep it safe.

3) Not being sure how it is relevant to the assignment brief. It may look very interesting and maybe you can find a purpose for it later. But if your "odds and ends" folder is bigger than the rest you are doing it wrong so go back and re-think what kind of information/sub-headings you are using.

 **Check relevance and time spent**

Re-read the assignment brief often to make sure you are doing what you are supposed to be doing.

Check your time allowance and don't go over it.

Once all the information is under a suitable sub-heading, and all sub-headings have enough information, you can think about a conclusion and, finally, an introduction. (How can you introduce something that doesn't exist yet?)

gain critical distance

Put it away for a few days (if you planned your time well you have included time to have a break and come back later). Read it later and see if is still makes sense to you. Was it as good as you remember it? Does anything need improving? How can it be improved in the time you have left?

proof read it

Use spell check (watch out for homophones) and be especially careful of technical terms. Look for sentences that don't read clearly and simplify them if necessary.

Have you answered the question and fulfilled the purpose? Does it meet the criteria?

hand it in on time

and congratulate yourself for being well organised.

evaluate your own process

What was easy and what was difficult? Why?

What went well and what went less well?

Were you always efficient in how you used your time and went about collecting and organising information?

What could you do differently next time for a better/easier result?

How to avoid cheating, even by accident

When you are asked to hand in work, it has to be your own. You should never hand in somebody else's work and pretend it is yours when you know it is not.

If you submit somebody else's work as if it were your own, that would be "plagiarism".

Plagiarism means stealing the thoughts, ideas, creative work or writings of another person. It would be cheating and stealing. It is against college regulations because it won't help you learn. Your tutor could refuse you a grade and can use the disciplinary code.

Test your understanding of this idea:

Which of the following examples seem to you to be cheating or stealing?

1) You have not finished your project. You need to hand it in soon. You get one from a student who has just finished the course and put your own name on it.

2) You are asked to research a subject and bring back the information you have found. You look in the library and on the internet. You find magazine articles, statements and pictures. You bring them back to the classroom. You use it to complete a project.

Answers and Explanations

The first is obviously not acceptable.

The second might also lead to trouble if you are not careful.

When you took the words or pictures from an internet site or a book, did you make sure everybody knew where they came from?

If you just pretended the work was yours when it wasn't, that would be obviously cheating. But if you use their work without giving the original person credit, that is also unfair. The reader might think it was all your work, instead of something you had found.

They might guess that it wasn't but think you were trying to pretend it was. It is better to remove all doubt and be very clear about who first wrote those words, or made that design, or drew that picture. Then you get credit for finding it and no danger giving the wrong impression.

Practical Work

Obviously, if you let somebody else do the work then handed it in that would be cheating. You may be asked to sign a "Certificate of authenticity" to make sure it is your own work.

But it is also obvious that you will receive help and advice from tutors, and possibly mentors, as you go through the process of making something. Your tutor will explain to you how much help of what kind you can receive before it becomes a problem, but it is also up to you to tell them when you submit it about any help you received outside college. If somebody at work or at home helps you with a practical project then you should tell your tutor so they can decide if that was too much help.

Pictures

Suppose you have to hand in a drawing of the four-stroke cycle in a petrol engine. It is very easy to get that from the internet. It may be permitted to download it and hand it in. But did you say which site you found it on, or does it look as if you are pretending it was yours? It is safer to name your source and avoid confusion. Then the tutor can look it up and see how much you have amended it or altered it, or whether you just stuck it in without adding anything to it to show you understood it.

If you only print it and hand it in, without even changing it, then the information has not really been processed by your brain. If you made your own drawings, the physical act of drawing would help you understand and remember.

By the way, if you want to find images that are free to use without worrying about copyright, try *http://search.creativecommons.org/* but note their rules on attribution.

Ideas

If you find a good recipe in an old book and pretend it is yours, that is obviously cheating. But if you say where you found it you can get credit for good research.

It is possible to find the answer to a homework question in a book which seems to tell you everything you need to know. If you take in that information and make it clear where you found it, then you may get credit for good research. Or at least for being very lucky. If you use it without naming the source, then you could be cheating and stealing. They are not your words, so you should give credit to the person who first wrote them.

Of course, you would learn more, understand better and remember more easily if you translate the original into your own words or drawings. So plagiarism is against college policy for two reasons

(a) it is unfair

(b) more importantly, it means you probably haven't learned anything.

Words

It is possible to download whole essays and projects from the internet. It might be useful to look at a few if you are stuck, but if you used even extracts without saying where you found them, then you are stealing and cheating. Even if it was by accident, you could end up in trouble because you can't prove it was an accident. If it looks like cheating, it will probably be treated as cheating.

These are various ways to credit your sources. If you are citing a fact an author told you about but not their direct words, you can just say:

> *Bains suggests that the most promising applications for hologram video are in medicine and industry*

But if you **quote directly** from a text then use quotation marks:

> "Cells must also, in some sense, know where they sit in relation to other cells." *(Dawkins 1995)*

or

> According to Dawkins , "Cells must also, in some sense, know where they sit in relation to other cells."

If it is a longer paragraph, you could 'indent' it like this:

> Radio and TV are distinctive means of communication with their own limitations and possibilities and their own particular techniques, and anyone who seriously wishes to sell work to the BBC must first become familiar with its existing output. - N. Longmate, *Writing for the BBC*

Remember that everyone's style of writing is unique, like their speaking voice. If you use someone else's words, it will not sound like you. The words will stand out as obviously not yours. It is safer to be honest and put quotation marks round them.

Also, tutors have access to as many web sites and text books as you do, and more experience in the subject. They will probably recognise the material you use. There are even search engines they can use to look through the internet to find that sentence. Your chances of getting away with deliberate deception are very small. And it would be a shame to look as if you were trying to deceive when you are just being careless or lazy. So use quotation marks, name your sources, and play safe.

Bibliography

Notice that bit in brackets (Dawkins 1995). If you are using a lot of quotations from several sources, you can list the authors and books in a bibliography at the end of your work. A simple version might include:

Author surname, followed by initials

Date of publication, in brackets

The title of the work - in italics or underlined

If the work is an article from a magazine or journal, write the title of the article, then the name of the magazine, followed by the date and page numbers. E.g. Useful facts for Homework Projects, National Student Monthly, May 2003, pages 10-12

Name of the publisher.

If it came from a website, you would put the URL :
www.howstuffworks.com

here are more rules about laying out bibliographies for science or literature, especially at level 3, and your tutor will advise you if necessary.

Group Work

If you work in groups to produce something between you, try to make sure you have agreement on who did what. When the work is handed in, don't let somebody who just hung around without contributing get credit for your efforts. Think about it before you start and ask for help if it gets complicated. But always make sure your work is your work, and somebody else's work is labelled as such.

If you have any questions about any of this information, make sure you ask your tutor before you go any further. Do not copy or cheat or steal other people's work. And do not give the impression that you have done it, even by accident.

You can borrow things and say where you borrowed them. You can quote people and say what you learned from them. Doing that is OK, but your work has to be your work.

Making bibliographies

If you are using a lot of quotations from several sources, you will obviously want a bibliography at the end of your work. The international standard (Harvard system) for a printed book is:

The author's surname followed by the initials (if more than one then in the same order as they appear on the title page).

Year of publication in brackets.

Title of the book in italics or underlined.

Edition of the book if there has been more than one (don't bother with only reprinting dates)

Volume number if there is more than one.

Chapter and/or page numbers (if only a part is used).

Place of publication or town of origin

Publisher's name

> Baron. S., Field, J. and Schuller, T. (2000) *Social Capital; critical perspectives* (Oxford, Oxford University Press)

In a less formal setting, you can abbreviate to OUP and in such an obvious case may not bother with the town. If the work is an article from a magazine or journal, write the title of the article, then the name of the magazine, followed by the date and page numbers.

> Ball, S.J. (1995*) Intellectuals or technicians?: the urgent case for educational theory,* British Journal of Educational Studies, 43,3,255-71

If it came from a website, you would put the URL :
www.howstuffworks.com

There are more rules about electronic books, speeches etc and if you are writing academic papers for a university you may need to consult them. They are freely available on the internet. Just google Harvard bibliography or try these sites as samples:

http://www.leeds.ac.uk/library/training/referencing/harvard.htm

http://www.sussex.ac.uk/library/infosuss/referencing/h_bibliography.s html

http://www.edgehill.ac.uk/tld/student/harvard/

http://www.shef.ac.uk/library/libdocs/hsl-dvc1.pdf

Formal letters and emails

5 Invented Mansions,

Example Rd.,

Cowtown,

West Sussex

BN23 5QT   20th November 2006

Dear Reader,

This letter is formal because we have never met. It shows you what a formal letter should look like and why it has to keep to certain patterns or rules. You can use it as an example.

The very first thing the letter does is to tell you what it is about. Never waste time. Get to the point. Why are you writing? What is the question or purpose? What do you want from them or what can you offer them? What do you want them to do about it? If you have to explain something fully then do so, but first make sure they know what it is going to be about and why they should bother to read it.

Firstly, you will notice I did not begin by saying "my name is ....." That will be obvious from the last line, when you sign it, so it always wastes time and sounds slightly amateur. You need to give the impression you know what you are doing, so they take you seriously and you get the right response. Formal letters do not have to be frigid, but they are wearing their best suit in court.

Of course, your name will only be obvious if they can read your signature, so you will notice I have typed mine under the handwriting, which is always a good idea. If you are not typing, then print it. Small matters like that make the reader's life easier. They are less likely to file the letter in the bin because you have annoyed them by being careless or selfish, expecting them to work it out from a scribble.

I have included a date and address. The reader will need to know where to reply. If they keep the letter on file for some time, may need to know how long they have it for. If it is part of an official complaint, or something that might go wrong and lead to trouble, like renewing a licence, then you may

need to prove who said what when. You will probably want to keep a copy.

If you type and store it on a computer, don't forget to back up your work. In such cases, you may also want to include at the top the name and address you sent it to, so there is never any doubt after the envelope has been thrown away. It might just turn up under a pile of papers on a desk one day, addressed Dear Sir, and nobody will know who owns it.

If you are writing to a bank of someone you pay for a service, then you may have an account number they need to identify you. This can be put at the very top of the letter, like this:

Dear Sir / Madam *(find their name first if you can),*

a/c 897460874678

 Or you can give the whole letter a title that helps them to identify who would deal with it, or what file to put it in:

Dear Sir,

parking for student transport

You don't have to do that, but it one more thing that helps them get to your point so they can act on your letter.

Finally, if it is not already obvious, make sure they know what it is you want from them. Information? By any particular deadline? Why do you need it by then? A refund? An apology? Or perhaps you are just writing to congratulate them on a job well done, and want no reply?

If you are complaining and expecting a refund or apology, then you can make your point firmly without being shrill and abusive. The letter is more likely to become 'lost' if you do. Don't bother making threats you won't carry out. If you say you will take them to court then be ready to do so. If you can't afford it, don't say it. They will probably not take you seriously anyway. On the other hand, there might be some kind of watchdog or ombudsman or official body they have to answer to. If they ignore your first letter you can send another with a copy to that official, and write on the letter 'copy to' so they know.

The usual abbreviation for that purpose is cc, which in old technology stood for 'carbon copy'.

If you are enclosing something, like an old bill or a photograph of damage caused by their driver, you may already have referred to it in the letter. Even if you have, it is customary to add below the signature a note to remind them – and perhaps to remind yourself to include it. You will see it at the bottom.

The final signature will either be yours faithfully or yours sincerely. Dear Sir is your faithfully. If you know the name you can use sincerely. In one sense, it doesn't seem to make any real difference, and few people could explain why that is the rule. However, if they know the rule and you obviously don't then you put yourself at a disadvantage. Don't wear your best suit with dirty shoes.

And don't waste time with complicated ways to sign off. Without being rude or curt, you can just say what you have to say clearly, then go. Unless, of course, you need to remind them, for example, that "I look forward to a new ticket before we leave on 26th of this month" or "unless we receive a satisfactory explanation we shall move out account elsewhere

I hope that helps.

Yours faithfully,

Sign here

Type your name here

enc: 3 photographs

PS:

This means post script (after the letter is finished) so **don't** use it. Use a word processor and add the idea to the letter before you print it.

Formal emails

An email is not a letter and it is a matter of choice whether you use a salutation (Dear Sir / Madam). For anything connected with a job application it could be safer.

Emails may seem informal but it is still a matter of business, so don't become too informal or friendly just because it feels like the sort of quick message you normally send to friends.

Don't use text speak.

Don't forget it can always be read by other people. It might be sent on to millions of people. If you don't want millions of people to read it, don't say it in an email.

Don't be tempted to send on the jokes that circulate on the internet. It is not what you are paid for (so you might face a disciplinary offence) and the other person might not find it funny. They might object to having their time wasted, or find it offensive, or sad. It might contain a virus.

If you write an angry email because someone has annoyed you with their message or actions, DO NOT PRESS SEND. Save a draft, read it again a day later and see if it is really what you want other people to read, including possible witnesses who did not witness what made you angry, only what you said. Mostly, they'll just think you're a troll.

How to make a presentation

You may have to make formal presentations for a number of reasons. It may be applying for jobs or training opportunities. At work, you might have to speak about a new idea, and perhaps persuade them to agree to it. In your private life, you might present your views at a formal hearing, tribunal or enquiry. Here are some pointers that will help.

general principles

preparing information

delivering information

General Principles

Be very clear about the topic and time limit. This may sound obvious, but if you are nervous about speaking it is easy to go wrong from the start by not checking the obvious details. What is the **purpose** of your delivery?

Be very clear what the audience need to know. There is no point speaking to people unless they want to listen. What do they need to know and why? Find out as much as you can about the audience.

Don't just fill in the time and risk boring them. Think about what they want and why they want it. Give them what they need and then they will listen and be grateful

Ask what would make it easier to understand your information. Would it help if you used a picture, handout, wall chart or OHP? If an example or image or chart makes things much easier to understand, the audience will be grateful.

Keep it simple and in logical order. Keep it simple, stick to the point, and look at it from the audience's point of view.

If you are showing people words on a display or handout, then bullet points are better than long explanations, visual charts better than tables of facts they can't digest. If something is really important, you may need to repeat it again in the conclusion, so they remember it. Can you choose a few key points at the end to summarise what you said?

Avoid annoying habits. Think of all the lessons or presentations you have sat through that annoyed or bored you. Think of the way information was presented, or the little habits the speakers had that got on your nerves – the coughing or mumbling or scratching or shuffling OHP slides that take too long to be up on screen or saying "OK?" every two sentences. Remember those habits, then don't do them.

Preparing Information

Start by selecting the general ideas that the audience need to know.

You can do this with mind maps, linear notes or tape recorded memos (q.v.). What counts is that you have a clear idea of the **structure and purpose** of any information.

For a general shape, use the classic advice:

Tell them what you are going to tell them

Tell it to them

Tell them what you told them

Prepare them with an introduction and end with a reminder of the main points or underline major conclusions.

Think carefully about **time limits.** Don't just gather information and then try to squeeze or stretch it. Choose it with the time limit in mind.

Use prompts, not scripts. If you just read a speech your voice will sound flat. You will tend to look down at the page instead of at the audience. You might lose your place.

Prompt cards, with short reminders of the main points in large letters, allow you to look up at the people with whom you are meant to be communicating.

Rehearse. You can try it alone, or into a tape recorder, or with a friend who can ask questions and make comments. Listen to what you say and how you say it, so that on the day your own voice sounds familiar to you and won't come as a nasty surprise. Is it light or breathy or fast? Can you change it with deeper breathing? Can you project more strength and confidence by looking up, breathing more deeply and speaking from the stomach instead of the chest?

Remember that rehearsals may be quicker or slower than the real thing. Will you speed up or slow down on the day? Don't push the time limit. Five minutes does not mean nine, fifteen does not mean twenty, and they might just cut you off...

Could you try a video record and watch your body language?

Delivering Information

Be ready. Turn up on time with all your notes. If you are using illustrations, and need to display them, are they big enough to be seen by everyone? Did you bring pins or bluetac? If you are using small illustrations, don't hand them round to be looked at then expect people to carry on listening to you. They will be distracted, waiting for the picture or even talking about it. Take control, let them look quickly, then carry on.

Look at them. Make eye contact before you start. Take control. Be friendly but in charge. Stare them out. If you are really nervous, and it is a large group, try looking slightly over their heads so they think you are looking at them but you can't see their eyes so it doesn't frighten you. But as soon as you can, if you can, look at them.

Speak to them. Don't spend ages shuffling your papers and wasting time. You get more nervous and they take against you before you even start. Stand up, say 'Good morning' (unless it is after 12) and get on with it.

Keep your place. If your prompt cards are in large font this is much easier. You can use a ruler to slide across them as you go, or move the last card across the next one to mark your place.

Invite questions, and be prepared to answer them. "I don't know" might be a good answer. It is better than trying to bluff and being found out.

Finish

It needs to be clear when you have finished. Your last statement should sound final. If it looks as if the script just fizzles out, at least say 'thank you' or in some other way signal that they can now applaud.

How to take part in discussions

It might be called an argument, a discussion or a debate. These words can be misleading. You need to be clear what kind of experience you are about to enter.

'Arguments' can mean an angry exchange when two people let out their emotions and even try to hurt each other. They get angry and might say things they don't really mean. You can appear to 'win' an argument buy shouting louder or being more aggressive or more hurtful.

'Debate' sometimes means an exchange of views to try to decide on the facts. But it can also mean a contest where you just want to win over an audience and get more votes. Then it can include dirty tricks and trying to trip up your opponent. Sometimes the winner is the one with the best jokes or the quickest reply to a putdown or heckle. That is a useful skill in some lines of work, but not a discussion.

Discussions work best when the people involved try to help each other explore an idea. There may be no right answer and there may be no winner. At the end of the event, perhaps the most you can hope for is that everyone has a clearer idea of what the problem is. You leave it wiser than you arrived, even if that means being less sure of yourself. Discussions are cooperative, and you score more highly by helping people than by tripping them up.

When you are taking part in a discussion, the general rules are that you should not:

> cut across another speaker

> speak while someone else is making a point

> state a fact without saying how it helps the argument

> accept an argument without enough evidence to support it

The fact that you have always believed something to be obvious does not mean it will make sense to everyone else. The fact that someone else's opinion annoys you or even seems ridiculous doesn't prove it to be wrong. The discussion has to be considerate and reasonable, but what does that mean? Basically, it means you need to help each other to look more closely at **the assumptions behind the opinions.**

For example, suppose you were a musician or actor or painter and the question was:

Should there be censorship of the creative artist?

Immediately, some will object that artists should be allowed to sing or paint or act on stage whatever they want. They need freedom of expression. The assumption here is that censorship prevents musicians, writers and painters from making interesting work, or from giving it to the public. Is this true? Is it a bad thing?

Someone might give examples of songs that were banned by the radio stations when they first came out. Those   objections now seem very old fashioned. They might mention films that were once considered shocking but now seem quite tame. It soon becomes clear that censors 10 or 20 years ago were very worried about words and scenes that now we consider harmless or even necessary. Artists come up with interesting work and censors try to stop it, but eventually they lose and the work gets seen or heard anyway. That makes them look ridiculous. In the long term, they seem to be losing a battle with creative people who make life more interesting, more free.

Someone might even mention other countries, where their standards are quite different to ours and they have very little freedom in our sense. They consider our music and films to be shocking, and even wicked. The assumption now is that we are free and they are not. But who is free to do what? Is it always what we want?

Soon, someone will point out that even people who argue for this freedom have their own personal limits. Is there anything you would not like to see on stage or screen? Is anything so violent or sexually explicit or sexually violent that it cannot be shown, even to 12 year olds or four year olds? If so, why not? Slowly, it will emerge that most people have a personal limit. They want to be free, but only so far. Or they want to be free, but don't want their little sister to see it. Or they want to be free but think nobody should be allowed to film that particular act and sell it on the internet. Why not?

Now the assumption is that maybe censorship has a role, because some things are too offensive or harmful. But:

Why should you not be offended?

How do you know it does any harm?

Are you just being prejudiced? If something is published or sung or acted and a lot of people are offended there may be a riot. Censorship limits freedom to keep the peace. That is why it is illegal to go round insulting people. If you did that and started a fight it would be you that got arrested, for starting the trouble. What sort of limits are we willing to accept to avoid annoying each other and living with constant rows and fights? And if someone has to draw a line, who should do it? How should they decide? Does anyone know how it is actually done at the moment?

And how exactly would a film or a song or an image harm someone? Would it give them nightmares? Would it make very young people afraid of the world and upset their development? Would it give them an unhealthy view of what as involved in adult life or sexual activity? How do you know? Who decides what is healthy? By what right? On what basis? What sort of assumptions are you making now?

As the ideas and information passes to and fro, you may find you have said something that later you cannot back up, or want to withdraw. The test of a good discussion is whether you can do that easily. Changing your mind may be progress. Finding out you were wrong may be progress, because you have learned more about what you think and why you think it. At one level, that makes you more aware of your own mind and how it works. At another level, if there is ever a debate, you are more likely to win it.

You may well find that if you keep questioning the assumptions it becomes very frustrating. Nobody can 'prove' anything at all and it gets too complicated. You may choose to accept some assumptions because you need some to work with. Fair enough. At this level you are only being asked to show that you can be reasonable, not right about everything. If you thought you were, you wouldn't be.

What is reasonable?

This might be a question about what you say or how you say it. It might apply to ideas or to your way of expressing them.

Suppose, for example, in talking about censorship, members of the group said something like this:

1) I am religious and I find bad language very offensive, so it ought to be censored to avoid offending me.

2) I am an atheist and I find religion offensive so it shouldn't be allowed to have special times on t.v. or radio. Religion in broadcasting or schools ought to be banned.

3) Some people's political views are extreme and they should not be allowed to repeat them in public.

4) I think all Dutch people have nasty habits and weird beliefs and ought to be kept out of this country.

5) God hates sinners and they will burn in hell.

6) My best friend was abducted by aliens but the newspapers won't tell his story. That is censorship.

Which of these opinions would strike you as 'reasonable'? Which of them seem to you to be expressed in a reasonable tone of voice? Everyone tends to think their own opinions are reasonable, however odd they may sound to someone else, so it would be difficult to convince them they were spoiling a discussion by being 'unreasonable'. There are three questions to settle and all of them are important.

1) Are they expressing a view so out of step with the majority that nobody will take them seriously?

That doesn't mean they are wrong. The first person to invent flying or railways or rock and roll or suggest votes for woman might have been in that position. Can we say that someone is unreasonable just because they are in a minority? Or is censorship designed so that the majority can live more peacefully?

2) Are they expressing a view that we cannot prove either way?

If I tell you it is raining, or that travelling by rail is cheaper than going by plane, you can check whether that is true. If I tell you my friend was abducted by aliens then how would you know? You don't have any way to check because you can't imagine what kind of evidence would be available that you and I would both accept.

One of the things you may have to settle in your discussion is what would prove something to be true. What kinds of statement can you prove and what can you only argue about? Which of the following can be settled by evidence and called a fact? Which is only opinion?

It is colder in Wales than in London today

It is more enjoyable to go on holiday to Wales than to Swindon

Global warming is a major threat to our lives

Cars should all be banned to avoid global warming

Petrol engines are more efficient than diesel engines

Chocolate is better than spinach

Becky is a cow

Swearing is wrong

Violence on t.v. will offend people

What kind of evidence would help you settle those questions and which of them cannot be settled by evidence? Sometimes it all depends on how you express yourself. What do you mean by 'better'? You could argue that trying to settle an argument without evidence is pointless. It might be 'unreasonable' because you can't use reason to settle it. But does that mean you can never have reasonable discussion about who is the best goalkeeper or singer, or whether we ought to eat whales or dormice for lunch?

Are they making 2 plus 2 equal five?

Part of the problem is how you apply evidence. You might have lots of facts but put them together the wrong way and jump to the wrong conclusion

The murder was carried out at 6a.m.

John was there at 6 a.m.

John committed the murder

Not necessarily, but if you were tired or lazy you might think so. Then John would spend time in the cells because of an unreasonable argument.

A **syllogism** is one good way to show if someone is using an argument that does not add up. You take three statements. Two of them are facts and the third is a conclusion

This table is made of wood

Wood burns

So this table will burn

The first two can be checked and tested. If they are true, then the third line is a logical conclusion.

Copper is a mineral

All minerals will burn

Therefore copper will burn

If the first two are true then the third line is a logical conclusion. If one of them is not true then the conclusion is wrong. It may or may not be true, but at last it is reasonable to say it, because you can check it out and agree on the evidence. If you can write out what people are saying to you this way, you can find out what is a fact and how the facts are supposed to connect. Turn their statements into a syllogism and show it to them so you can both check it. Try the following. Warning – some may be true.

This cylinder contains gasses

Oxygen is a gas

So this cylinder contains oxygen

Megan has red hair

All redheads have bed tempers

So Megan must have a bad temper

David Beckham is a footballer

All footballers are athletes

So David Beckham is an athlete

Leslie is a biker

Some bikers are women

Therefore Lesley is a woman

My goat is called Fred

Grass is green

Therefore my goat eats grass

Water freezes at O° Centigrade

This liquid freezes at O° Centigrade

Therefore this liquid is water

Goats eat green things

Grass is green

Therefore Fred eats grass

Spinach contains iron

Iron is good for you

Therefore spinach is good for you

Spinach is supposed to be good for you

I hate spinach

So it can't be good for me

Caffeine is a drug

Coffee contains caffeine

Therefore coffee is a drug

This metal bar is made if iron

Iron is good for you

Therefore this metal bar would make good soup

I am unemployed

This Bulgarian has a job in my area

Therefore I am unemployed because of EEC immigration policies (so I ought to thump him)

How much of that is checkable and how many of the connections are logical? If you took the statements people are making in the discussion, which of the syllogisms above seem closest to the way they are thinking? Can you use syllogisms to get people to agree on what is 'reasonable'?

Curriculum Vitae and interviews

A curriculum is the course you follow. Your *curriculum vitae* is the story of your life so far. Vitae = life, as in vitality. It helps if the c.v. shows some.

These pages show one way of laying it out. There are alternatives, and some employers will have a preferred model or even a form to fill in instead. If you are free to design your own, what matters is that you follow a clear logic and make it perfect for the purpose.

If consulting an expert, always consult more than one then make up your own mind who to believe. You could try *http://www.bbc.co.uk/radio1/onelife/work/index.shtml?cvs#topics*.

A c.v. has to impress the reader even before they read it, or they may not. It needs clear design, to lead them straight to the information that will impress them. Don't waste their time. Many employers will throw poor c.v.s in the bin without reading them. The reasons, in order, are usually:

1) Wrong spelling of curriculum. Use it in full for the title. If you shortened it to c.v. in a covering letter then remember the dots for abbreviation, or it looks sloppy.

2) Poor physical design. That might mean confusing or thoughtless layout, poor quality paper or printing, trying too hard and showing off with fancy typefaces etc. Keep it simple. Keep it adult - leave out the teddy bears and Microsoft border designs.

3) Spelling, grammatical or typing errors. Even one might be enough. If you were faced with fifty applicants for one job would you read all the c.v.s? What's the quickest way to throw some away and save yourself time. Always think of the person reading them. Try to help them, not annoy them.

There are lots of professional services offering help to create the perfect c.v. They can be expensive. This section may save you having to use them, but you may find it useful to ask a few other people to read it over before you send it. Can you find someone who actually works in the right industry?

C.V.s always tell the truth. Employers can check qualifications. If you lie on a c.v. you can be fired later. But the truth can perhaps be polished and presented in the best light. Use your verbal skills and good free advice to find the best way to explain what you have been doing and why. Experience that appears to be negative or unimportant might, if you present it properly, support your claim to be suitable.

> *I have never had a job before but I worked for my uncle in the holidays. I was mostly moving stuff about but sometimes I kept a list of where it went.*

Try

> *Shared responsibility for stock control in busy warehouse/*

Instead of

> *Spent most of the summer playing with my band in local gigs but also worked in a shop selling drums and sometimes in a supermarket. I found some places and got*

my brother to lend us some speakers and drive us and sometimes I argued about how much we got paid.

Try

Responsible for booking venues and organising events for local group. Organised transport and technical back up and negotiated contracts. Retail experience includes direct customer service in both music and x industries.

Think about layout and visual appeal:

Curriculum Vitae

John Smith

*This could be John Martin Smith or even **Smith**, John Martin*

15 Beale Street,

Lowton,

JN1 2TA

01493 67496

mobile 0776 874 9837

JS@jsmith.co.uk

Could be laid out like this:

John Smith

15 Beale Street, Lowton, JN1 2TA

01493 67496   mobile 0776 874 9837 <u>JS@jsmith.co.uk</u>

A one-sentence summary of what makes you so fascinating, important, useful, worth the time to read about. It has to be true but eye catching and exactly right for that particular reader/opportunity. It wants a lot of work to get it just right. Revise it and try it out on other people. It could be in a box (choose the box icon on the formatting toolbar in Word).

An experienced guitarist/songwriter who has worked with groups in local venues, had two songs recorded and travelled for session work.

Born 15th September 1987 Wigan (British and American citizenship).

They may also need your age if it is relevant to the job. They could, of course, work it out, but don't annoy them by making them work harder.

Education.

The usual layout is:

Name of school	*location*	*years*
City College	Newport	2005 - 6

Greyfriars PRU   Hove   2001-5

Only use schools from secondary upwards. This shows the most recent first, as it is probably the most impressive. Check if any form wants them the other way round.

Qualifications

List those that look good and include those you are about to take (for the latter, under grade, put tba = to be advised).

Subject   grade   date

You can't lie about what you have but you can choose not to mention anything with a very low grade. If it doesn't help you may want to leave it out. On the other hand, a grade E in Maths is still a grade in something very difficult, so could be worth using. Grade F in RE is possibly less useful. On the other hand, include anything non-academic if its adds to the impression. First Aid?

Experience.

What can you offer here? Remember, you don't have to lie to make the truth more persuasive. Your previous jobs may not seem relevant directly but they might include some responsibility or initiative you can bring out.

Usually, if there is no form to fill in, you would lay it out something like this:

post   employer   address   dates

'Post' tells them what the job was called. If the title doesn't make it obvious what you were doing, you could add a column that says 'responsibilities' and tell them. This is where you bring out all the good qualities you showed.

Dates usually start from the latest and work backwards, although some forms work the other way round so check.

Some students have had no full-time jobs. Only bother to include any part-time work if it helps to show that you have certain qualities. Being fired for turning up late is a good reason not to mention it. Being asked to take on certain responsibilities is a good reason to include it, and 'big it up'.

Some people with a full-time record have embarrassing gaps for various reasons. If it is only a few months, for illness or unemployment, perhaps you can just ignore it. If you had a lot of jobs in a short time, you might be able to cover it with a single sentence

A variety of semi-skilled and manual jobs whilst saving to be a student.

or

A variety of semi-skilled and manual jobs whilst travelling in Europe.

They may, of course, ask for details for security purposes. They may check.

Referees

name

status or title

address

tel

email

You want **two** people who will say good things. Ask them first. If they won't say good things, find someone else, but one usually has to be the last college or employer.

Sign: (nothing too flashy or illegible – you can make a really good one and scan it in?)

Date:

****

Think about fonts and layout.

> Arial or Calibri 12 point is usually good - not too flashy.

> You can use 14 point if you have lots of space and need to fill it up.

Try to lay it out so you don't have stray words running over the page. Try to get it all on one or two pages that look full and attractive – don't have two pages of large print and then just one line on page 3.

Being interviewed for a job or college place

the application and advert

sources of information

getting there

appearance

entering

them and us

answering and asking questions

moving on

Whether for a job or a college place, there are certain ideas basic to all interviews. The first of these is that you have to prepare. This does not mean just working out precise answers to predictable questions. They may ask you something you could not have expected, but if you have organised your information properly you can usually make a sensible reply.

The application and advert

First, remind yourself what you applied for and what you said. Read the advert or course description very carefully. Are there any clues to what sort of person they are looking for and why?

What have you already said about yourself? Have you got plenty of examples or evidence to prove it was true? Can you think of something you have done to illustrate your best qualities or experience? Do you need to write it down.

When you have worked out what qualities they are looking for you can try to match what you have said and what you have done to prove you are the right person. Then you will have something to say whatever they ask you, and can look for a chance to say it even if they don't ask. Knowing you have those facts ready will help you feel and look more confident.

Sources of information

Don't go to an employer or college without studying them first. You can start with the internet or prospectus. if you can show you have researched them it will do you no harm. Maybe the information you find will suggest questions they might ask, or suggest one for you to ask them.

Do you know anyone who has been there? What do they say about it? Can their opinion be trusted?

Getting there

Use a map or the internet to make sure you know exactly where it is and how to get there. There is no excuse for getting lost or being late. Prepare and allow for possible hold ups. If your smart phone is not charged, use a college computer check these sites:

http://www.uk.map24.com/

http://uk2.multimap.com/

http://www.theaa.com/travelwatch/inc/planner_main_redirect.jsp

http://www.viamichelin.co.uk/viamichelin/gbr/tpl/hme/MaHomePage.htm

http://www.nationalrail.co.uk/

http://www.tfl.gov.uk/tube/

http://www.thetrainline.com/default.asp?href=&T2ID=4585_2005 91292153

http://www.highways.gov.uk/

http://www.couchsurfing.com/

As with exams, it can be unsettling to arrive too early, but it is easier to use up time with a rest, or by soaking up the atmosphere, than it is to arrive breathless and have to apologise for keeping them waiting.

Appearance

It is not always easy to guess the dress code that is likely to apply. You want to feel you fit in and look as if you have made the effort. If you are not sure what they will expect you can always ring and ask. If you don't want to ask the person who will be interviewing you, there may be an assistant in Personnel or Admissions who can help.

If in doubt, it is safer to be too formal than too informal. It is easier to remedy at the last moment and less likely to look careless, cocky or immature.

Think about how you will look and sound to them. Is there anything you do, perhaps unconsciously, that is irritating? Do you slouch or say "umm" too often or scratch yourself? Ask an honest friend or a tutor to advise you.

Entering

Try not to fall over the carpet. If you do, don't blame the carpet. Just get up and pass it off with a smile as one of life's little incidents. Things do go wrong, so expect it but be ready to overcome the problem calmly.

Are there more people than you expected? Fewer? Is the room larger or smaller? Are they further away? Do they look tired or fed up? Whatever you find, you have to deal with it, so don't be upset because the scene that meets you is not the one you expected. Walk in as confidently as you can. If you show a little nervousness, that is quite understandable, but at least you can try to look friendly and ready for a business-like conversation.

Them and Us

Not all interviewers are aggressive monsters who want to trip you up. Remember that interviewers are also people.

They may be as nervous as you are. It might be the first time they have ever interviewed anyone. You should go in expecting to get on with people, then you probably will.

When you have gone, they will need to think about what you said and look for evidence they you are right for the job or place. You need to have left in their minds enough evidence for them to feel confident that you are a safe choice, not someone who might let them down.

The key here is evidence. Don't just tell them with a big smile that you 'have always been interested in ' or ' would be very good at' something. Prove it. Dig out from the ideas or c.v. or application form something you have done that shows the quality or ability they are looking for. Leave them with evidence they can think about.

Try to speak at a reasonable pace - not to slow and ponderous but not too quick and nervous. Listen to your own pitch and volume –

is it nervously low or high? Can you deliberately change it?

Keep to the point. If you hear yourself starting to ramble it may be better to stop now. If you think of another point later you can always come back to it and make sure you tell them before you leave. They won't mind. Why should they? Pay them the compliment of treating them as reasonable people.

Answering and asking questions

They won't only ask you what you expect to be asked. They may not ask you anything you have prepared. Be prepared for that. You might get a friend to ask you some questions before you go, and throw in something really unexpected to test out your reactions. On the day, you are entitled to think before you reply. Get used to doing so. Use the information you have prepared to respond to them. Think about what they are asking and about what you want them to know. Then try to match the two as you reply. It may help to have a file with you and hold it. Have a pen or pencil ready to note down anything that crops up so you can come back to it later. You can cross off points as they are dealt with.

Some questions are factual and require only short answers. Others are more open – they are giving you a chance to say a bit more. Be ready to take the initiative. Expand and use the opportunity to make useful points. Make sure you answer the question they actually asked, but at the same time this may be your chance to lead them into areas where you feel comfortable or have points to make.

If they mention something you claim on your c.v. or statement, don't just say "yes, that's right" but expand on it. Use that opportunity to add something to show why it is evidence that you are suitable. What do you normally do that makes people respect or trust you?

If invited to ask questions, ask at least one. If they have genuinely covered everything you wanted to ask in the previous conversation then at least check through your notes and tell them so – don't just look unprepared. If you have lots of questions, try to reduce them to the three most important. Cross them off as you ask them. If you are not invited, but the question is important, make sure you ask before you leave.

In a job interview, your first question should never be about hours or salary or holidays. It is better to start by asking about prospects. For a course, you might want to ask about pass rates for pervious years. As information is given to you, don't be shy about making notes. It shows you are actively listening to them.

There is always the possibility that someone will just say "tell me about yourself". Be prepared with facts about yourself that seem relevant to that job/course and prove you have the qualities they are looking for. There is a difference between boasting and just stating the facts in your own interest. Think in advance about evidence and your achievements and interests and how they make you suitable for this place. Explain it to a friend, or tape recorder, or a mirror, or a passing ant. But think about it before you go in.

If the answer to any question counts against you, because something in your past was a mistake, then it is often better to tell the truth bluntly than to waffle or try to avoid the issue. You should have expected the problem and prepared a suitable explanation.

Moving on

When you have finished, there is nothing more to do but to prepare for the next interview. It is not unusual to attend several interviews before you find what you are looking for, so don't be disheartened. Each one is an opportunity to learn how to be interviewed. Think about what went well and how you can adapt and improve for the next one. If you think you have made mistakes you can learn from them for next time.

No matter how many times you may have to go through the process, remember that other people are also going through it, stay positive and take heart from the fact that being interviewed is better than not being interviewed, so you must have done something right to get that far. Try to work out what is was and do it again.

Good luck

Revision, memory and exams

revision must be active

revision must suit your style

improving memory

time and effort has to be managed

taking the exam

revision must be active

Memory can be short term or long term.

What you store in your short term memory may be forgotten again in a day or two. Most of what you read will just slide across your short term memory then disappear again very quickly.

To get information into your long-term memory you must have to do something with it. With information, you must use it or lose it. The more you use it, the more it lodges in your long term memory. If you just sit and stare at it, nothing happens.

One way to use information is to turn linear notes into **mind maps.** These are also covered in an earlier section, but note that, when used for revision:

- You may want one for each separate 'topic' or 'theme'. Can you actually identify topics or themes clearly from your notes? If not, do you need advice?

- More important ideas will be nearer the centre and less important items will be nearer the edge. Does making the map clarify relative importance?

- The links between the key concepts will be immediately apparent because of their proximity and connection. This visual image may stay in the mind longer than a page of words and could be sketched in the margins of an answer sheet.

- In order to construct a good mind map, you need to thoroughly understand a topic and the links between different items. This means you have processed the information to a deep level so it is more likely to be fixed in your memory.

If you don't like mind maps, you can use **flash cards** (questions with notes for an answer carried in your pocket). You can share these with others, perhaps even making some each and swapping them. Or you could use a **mobile recorder** to test yourself, either by recording your ideas for checking later or by having model answers ready to play if you get stuck. What else are 'phones for? Could you share the process with a few friends by texting, emails or even a shared web site with FAQs?

Wht is a proton? \Is it (a) hair trtmnt (b) Elctrc car (c) Villain in Dr. Who (d) Cntr of nucleus? xx

revision must suit your style

You should know by now what kind of student you are. Visual, aural, kinaesthetic? Left or right brain? If not, see first sheets 25 and 26. You also know from those sheets that sometimes learning methods have to be adjusted to suit particular preferences. Would you learn most by reading notes or by writing them out again? By looking at them or by talking about them? Maybe they ought to be recorded so you hear them played back to you? Should you be sitting still and quietly or walking about playing music? Use what you learned from those sheets to make it easy for yourself. Take control and manage the process. If you just stare at a page it will just stare back, but it won't speak to you.

Improving memory

Things that appear forgotten are often available but not accessible. They are in our memory somewhere, but we cannot get at them. We need cues to find the memory; the better the cues the better the chances of a successful retrieval. These are some ideas you could try:

understanding

If you can see how an idea links up with other ideas, it will be easier to remember it. People often remember an idea wrongly because they never really understood it. When revising it, try explaining it to others to make quite sure you really understand it. A small group can take it in turns to explain key ideas to each other, sharing the load and correcting any misunderstandings and careless phrasing. For exams, you don't just want the idea – you want the idea wrapped in words that can be written down quickly and recognised by the examiner.

organisation

Formulation is important because in exams you don't just want knowledge but knowledge is repeatable form – in usable chunks you can get down on paper in a time limit. You need it wrapped in the right words that come back to you on time. That is more likely if you have organised the information.

Work out the logical structure and use headings and sub-headings; underline key words; construct mind maps; talk to others about it. Get used to seeing it from several angles, so you are not thrown by a devious question to which you really know the answer.

And make sure you understand how the exam questions work.

What sort of exam is it? Multiple choice? Open ended questions? Questions that start easy and get harder as they go on? A choice of questions? Trick questions?

You can't predict what they will ask, but you can study past papers to see what kind of questions they will be. What sort of language do they use? Are there any typically awkward ways they may dress up a simple question? What clues do they give you as to the kind of answer they are seeking? There is no point knowing a great deal about something unless you know it in a way that is suitable for this purpose.

Imagery and association

a) Some people use pictures or diagrams to help them remember. For example, in Geography GCSE you may learn about factors that decided where people made settlements. This childish diagram sums them up.

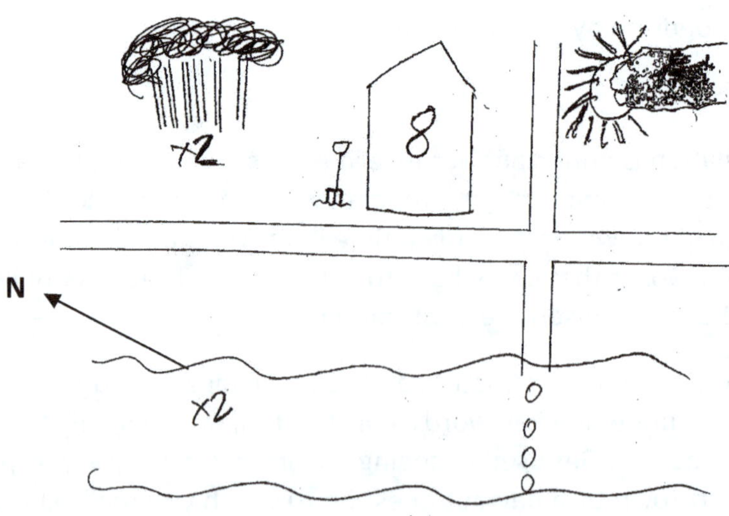

There are 8 reasons why that house might be there. The trees provide 2 reasons (shelter and building materials) and the river provides 2 reasons (water and a convenient crossing point). It is also situated at a crossroads and the drawings of a fork and a sun behind the clouds remind you about soil condition and climate. The arrow showing North reminds you about aspect (it can face the sunny side and away from cold winds).

b) Some people will find it easier to use words, and could more easily remember BWCSCASC (building materials, water, climate, soil, crossroads, aspect, shelter, crossing) especially if they could make up a sentence to help them, like

Buildings

Will

Create

Settlements,

Choosing

A

Suitable

Corner

In earlier times, defence was also a major consideration. How could you add that to the drawing and the sentence above? BWCSCASDC = "suitable defensible corner" ?

c) Some people remember information best in the room where they learned it. That is not much help if you are taking an exam in a different room, but perhaps you can carry your own 'memory room' in your head? Imagine a room. Get used to looking at it with your eyes closed. Then start to file key ideas in certain parts of the room. Put them where they are easily 'seen' and recalled. Depending on how your mind works, that may be top left or bottom right. It might be behind a cupboard. Experiment. See what works best for you. Then, wherever you are, just close your eyes and remember that familiar room full of useful ideas.

mnemonics

If you don't think visually, you may prefer one of these methods to help bring things to mind.

1. *Rhymes* – 30 days have September, April, June and November.

2. *Acronyms* – letter cues to help you recall more complex material, e.g. laser' = **L**ight **A**mplification by **S**timulated **E**mission of **R**adiation.

3. *Acrostics* – sentence or expressions whose first letters serve as cues for recalling specific material, e.g. Richard of York Gave Battle In Vain (colours of the rainbow in order. Buildings will create settlements, choosing a suitable defensible corner?

Whatever you use, you will find that active learning produces better results than just reading or listening passively. Also when using imagery or mnemonics, you can make your picture or rhyme as unusual, colourful, silly or rude as possible to help recall.

time and effort has to be managed

Studying has to be fitted in with other responsibilities, which may include paid work. You have to pace yourself and get a suitable rhythm.

If you need to remember large amounts of information, then spread it out over several short sessions. If necessary, reduce the amount per session until it feels manageable. You can build up to larger amounts again later. And before you even start, try to make sure you are only learning what you need. Do you need to know everything about everything on the syllabus or can you reduce the load by knowing what will NOT be examined? What is essential and what is only useful if you have the spare time? Sort your files out first so it is easy to find what you need to revise. This puts ideas in a rough order and helps jog your memory. It will save wasted time later.

Take short breaks between sessions, or you will become less efficient and just waste the time you are spending on it.

Try to get some exercise during revision time. Your body's reaction to exam stress is to generate extra nervous activity which exercise will burn off. It will also increase the blood supply to your body, including your brain so you'll think more clearly.

taking the exam

Take the Test Test (files 57 and 58). Remember what you learned from it. Also find out if there are any special rules about how you should write the answers? Start each on a new page or always carry straight on? Do you have to tick off which ones you answered?

The night before, stop revising. Put in one bag all the things you will need (pens, pencils, proof of identity, any formal exam or candidate numbers, any books you can take in, sweets that won't rustle, glasses, money for fares, watch, map of the place if unfamiliar etc.). Then go to the pictures or for a meal with someone who can keep you occupied in thinking about something else. Home for an early night.

On the day, eat a decent breakfast of the kind of food that will digest slowly and give you energy through the day. Not too much sugar, salt or caffeine – if your high runs out mid-exam you can't restock, so eat to stay even (see files 27-29)

Know where and when (it's all in your bag). Don't arrive too early and hang about feeling nervous, but make sure you won't be held up and arrive late.

Turn off your mobile.

If you feel nervous, tell yourself that is quite natural. So does everyone else. It helps to get the adrenalin going, which is useful within reason. But if it feels like you are breathing with your chest then try breathing from your belly. That reduces adrenalin. Stretch your muscles and breathe deeply. When doing so, try to stretch your fingers without removing anyone's eyes or cleaning their ears for them.

Read the questions. If there are choices to be made, select them. Once you have selected it, make sure you understand it before you rush to answer it. Use notes in margins or on a scrap page to prepare your answer. You may have some diagrams or mnemonics to work from, but if not don't panic. If other people start scribbling down their answers quickly they might be making mistakes by not reading the question properly. When you are ready, then go for it.

other sources

Google 'revision' with or without the name of your subject. Choose all pages then only pages from the UK. Try these examples:

http://www.bbc.co.uk/schools/gcsebitesize/

http://www.schoolhistory.co.uk/lessons/impactofwar/wwi recruitment.html

http://www.s-cool.co.uk/default.asp

http://www.schoolhistory.co.uk/gcselinks/

If you think you are now ready, maybe you should take the test on taking tests - version one is easier than version 2. Which would you prefer?

Test on taking tests - version one

You have five minutes to finish this test. No pressure, but if you fail you are going to feel very embarrassed.

You cannot pass without carrying out all the instructions carefully.

***

Do not talk to anyone and do not look at anyone else's paper.

Use a black or blue pen, not a pencil or any other colour.

Read all the questions before you write any answers

***

1) Print your full name on the top of the paper.

2) Write the name of your course underneath it.

3) What is the opposite of (a) genius? (b) success?

4) Write down the last four letters of the alphabet, in reverse order.

5) Add up the number of letters in your full name.

6) Multiply this by ten, then by the number of letters you wrote in answer 3.

7) Shout out "I have written down the number".

8) Shout "Ho, ho ho" four times.

9) Now go back and answer question one only – ignore the rest.

TEST TEST - version two

Do not speak with anyone else during this test.

Use a black or blue pen on official answer paper. All workings and notes must be shown on that paper. Write the number of the question in the left-hand margin.

Read all instructions very carefully, and read all the questions before you write any answers.

1) Write your name and course title at the top of the page.

2) Write your date of birth in numerical form (eg. 14/2/1986)

3) Write the letters of the alphabet in reverse order.

4) Circle each fourth letter.

5) Add the total number of circled letters to the total of the numbers in your date of birth. NB-14th Feb=14/2=14+2=16 NOT 1+4+2=7

6) Divide the total so far by 3 and then double it and write down the answer.

7) Shout out "I have written down the number."

8) Shout "Ho Ho Ho" four times.

9) Now go back to the beginning and do questions 1 and 2 only.

Hand in both question and answer papers.

See next page for feedback.

After the event, ask yourself:

Did you read all the questions first?

How did you feel when you saw the paper?

What was the worst part of it – the language, the grammar, natural nerves?

Would exams be less frightening if you were used to their language? How could you achieve that?

How likely is it that you would lose marks in a test even though you know the answer? Why? What can you do about it?

What kind of learner does best in this particular test? What are the main criteria for succeeding in your own qualifications?

Part two

Using language efficiently and effectively

Why is writing more difficult than speaking

Written language does not contain as many choices as spoken language. It doesn't have:

non-verbal communication (nvc) – gestures, winks, nods, shrugs, facial expressions.

tone of voice - it can be very difficult to write down in words what a certain tone of voice actually meant. In speech, we can use one word with lots of different tones to have lots of different meanings. How many ways can you say "hello" or "sorry" that mean different things?

feedback – a chance to see how people react as you speak. When you are writing, you have to finish and post it before you get any idea if it makes any sense to them or whether they have understood.

Also, when you are writing, you have to stop and think about

sentences and paragraphs

spelling

layout

Choices

NVC is often much more subtle than words. There are small movements of the eyes or eyebrows that give the impression you don't entirely believe someone, or might want to come over and talk to them. In crowded rooms, at parties, when talking to strangers, we often watch body language to tell if people are friendly. Even in texting, we might use smileys to include a facial expression – we can't manage without body language.

To find exactly the right word you need a lot to choose from. That is why
You might need a thesaurus (see Tools of the Trade). But even if you find the right word, how do you know what it means to the person you send it to? Ask different people to draw you a spiral. Which of these will they offer you?

 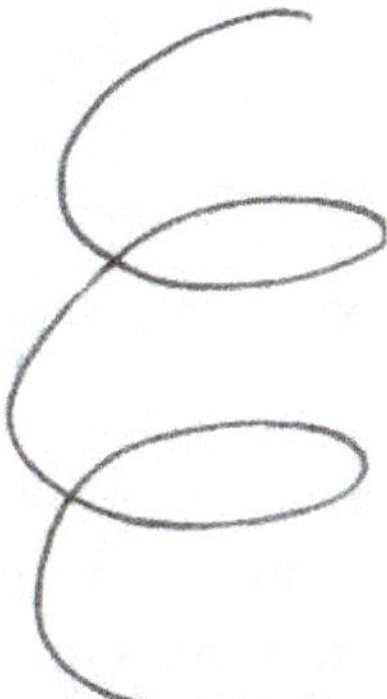

What is the difference between a spiral and a coil? What do they all mean by old, beautiful, sensible? If you don't know what a word will mean to your reader, it is harder to choose the right one. If they were standing in front of you, it is easier to tell if they get the wrong idea, because you can get instant feedback. If you are stuck, you can wave your arms or draw a picture or point to something. You can't do this when you write, so you have to think more carefully about what to say and how to put it.

Rules for writing

On top of that, all written language has its own rules. There are rules about how to make letters or reports. None of that matters when you are speaking. Other sections will explain what they are and why they matter when you are writing. You have more to think about, so it is harder to get ideas down on to paper. That is why some people find it easier to speak their ideas into a recorder first, then change them to fit the rules as they write it down.

Register

This is a term for how formal or informal you are.

Good morning, please come in.

Watcha. Come in bruv.

Alright? In.

These all say the same thing, but in different 'voices'. You wouldn't want to use the wrong register in the wrong situation. Most people find it easy to know the right register when they are speaking. A look on their face (nvc) or their tone of voice will tell you if you got it wrong. It takes a bit more thought when you are writing. Would you end a letter with *yours faithfully, yours sincerely* or *laters?*

The first thing to realise is that writing is more difficult than speaking for everybody, for very good reasons. You send ideas to someone in writing and make them understand very well with a bit of practice. But you need to start by understanding the problem and then feeling positive about beating it. It may help to know where the English language came from, and how it became so complicated. You can find that out next.

What is 'English' anyway?

Before people arrived, when it was just lions and earwigs, nothing had a name, because there was nobody here to speak about anything. Then, slowly, some human tribes came this way. As different groups settled in, speaking different languages, they started to name things and talk about them, and words came here from all over the world.

The first group to come were Celts. Their tribe were called Britons and that is why we now call the country Britain. They used their language to name places and things and a lot of the words they used are still with us today. Places with Celtic names include London, Crewe, Avon and Dover and the rivers Thames and Ouse.

Sometimes you wouldn't know a place was named by the Celtic language unless you knew what old words meant. For example:

Old word	meaning	place name
aber	mouth of a river	Aberdeen
car	castle	Carlisle
combe	hillside	Ilfracombe
strath	valley.	Strathclyde
pen or ben	mountain	Ben Nevis
loch	lake	Loch Lomond
inch or innis	island	Innis Sark
cairn	rocky hill or heap of stones	Cairngorm

A lot of these examples come from Scotland or Ireland. That is because the original inhabitants with the original language carried on living in these places for a long time, without being invaded very often, so the names lived on into our century. The language of Scotland, and Ireland – a version of Celtic known as Gaelic – is still spoken there in schools. Welsh is still the first language in many Welsh areas. In other places, new arrivals changed the names to something in their own language. But there are still words used today that have come down to us from that original group and are used by everybody. They include gull, bard, clan, slogan, whisky, reel, shanty and brogue.

Latin, Greek, Arabic and Hebrew

The next group to arrive were Romans. Their Empire included the top of Africa, large areas of the Middle East and most of Europe. They came for a quick look around with Julius Caesar in 55BC and within 100 years they were living in most of the country as far as the Welsh and Scottish borders. London was renamed Londinium. Romans spoke Latin. They stayed a long time and a lot of words you now think of as English originally came from Latin, including salary, mile, paternal, barbarian and flower.

At first. they had their own religion with their own gods – Mars was one of them. When you eat a Mars Bar you are eating a Roman god of war. Later, they became Christians. The Pope still lives in Rome, and the language of the Catholic Church for hundreds of years afterwards was Latin. Pray and prayer come from Latin words. The Bible wasn't originally in Latin. The Old Testament was written in Hebrew, and cherub is a Hebrew word. The New testament was first written in Greek, then translated into Latin. Angel is a Greek word.

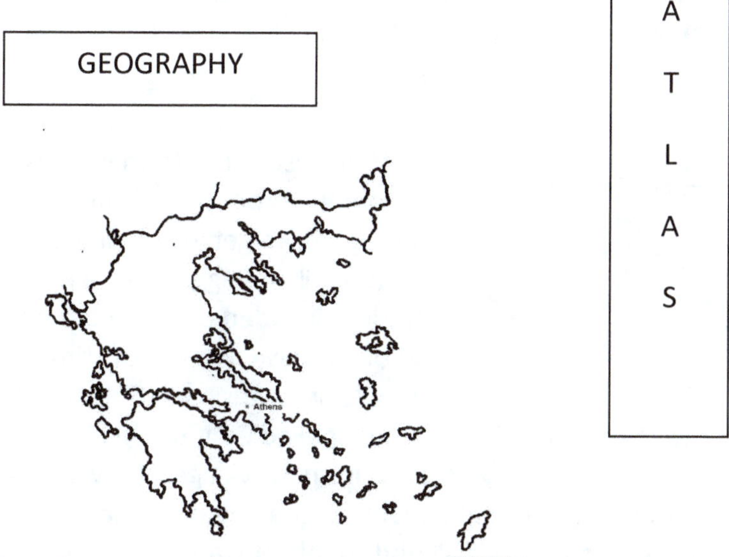

When somebody has a good idea, then other people will use it, and they will call that idea by the name it was first given, whatever language it may be. Lots of new inventions came from Latin, but a lot also came from Greek. Greek gave us words for arithmetic, geometry, physics and biology. A list of books is called a bibliography, from the Greek word biblios = book. They also gave us words like theatre and atlas, but words like zero and algebra came from Arabic. Good ideas spread, and the word in the original language spreads with them.

Old English and Danish

When the Romans went home, the next people to arrive were German. Their tribes had different names – Angles, Saxons, Jutes and Frisians – but their languages were all from the same place and we tend now to call it all Anglo-Saxon. This is what became Old English, and the word England came from the Angles. From this language we get words like father, mother, plough, numbers from one to ten and days of the week. Thursday is named after their god Thor and Wednesday after their god Woden. Husband and wife are Old English words, although they took them from Danish .

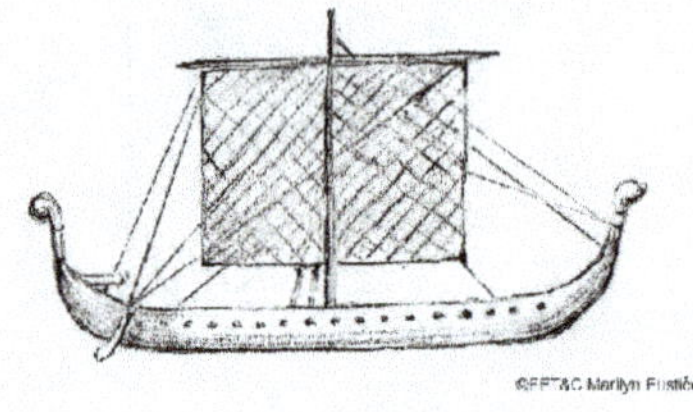

Settlers also came from what is now Denmark. From their Danish language we get words like law, skin, skull and egg. Later, when Vikings invaded the island, they also spoke Danish. For a short time, the whole area was part of the Danish Empire, under King Knut (sometimes spelled Canute). In places like Whitby and Derby, the *–by* part is Danish for village. The word *beck* is Danish for brook, so if that appears at the end of a place name (Troutbeck) you know it has a good supply of water and used to be Danish.

French

French words arrived in 1066 with the Normans. Parliament is a French word, and so are duke, duchess, baron and prince. Marriage is a French word, and dandelion (dents de lion, or lion's teeth). They became the next rulers and for a while, some of the Anglo-Saxons became their slaves, but then the two groups joined together and families from the two groups married each other. Old English and French words joined together to make a complicated mixture and that is what eventually became modern English.

Because so many new groups brought their own words for things that had already been named, modern English will often have two words when most other languages only have one.

From German (Old English)   **from French or Latin**

ask   enquire

blunder   error

bright   radiant

burial   funeral

buy   purchase

earthly   terrestrial

fearful   timid

roomy   spacious

Modern additions

That was nearly a thousand years ago. Lots more words have arrived since then. It may have been people who came to live here and bought the word with them. Or it may have been people from these islands who went abroad and brought the word back when they came home. Often, the word came because somebody had a good idea and people who copied it used their name for it.

Between 1600 and 1950, around 20 million people left the UK to go abroad and live in what was then The British Empire. Between 1950 and 2000, about one million people from what used to be The

Empire came to live in the UK. That is a lot of people swapping ideas and words.

Italian	corridor, opera, quarantine, piano, miniature, spaghetti
Turkish	coffee, kiosk
Malay	bamboo, sago, caddy (a measurement of tea), amok
Persian	bazaar, caravan, orange
Languages spoken in India, Pakistan and Bangladesh	shampoo (Hindi 1762,rrived via Mr. Mohammed in Brighton), bungalow, pyjamas, guru, chutney, pundit, calico, buddha, yoga, khaki.

Chinese	tea (and char)
Romany	pal, gaffer, chav
Czech	robot
Russian	vodka
Hungarian	coach, goulash

African languages   safari (swahili), jumbo

Dutch	trek, poppycock
German	kindergarten, noodle and lager
Finnish	sauna
Modern French	crèche, denim, cafe, chauffeur
Nahuatl (Aztec)	chocolate, avocado
Indian language of the Incas	potato (via Spanish)
Indian language of Tobago	tobacco

Because Latin and Greek were the words used by the people who invented science, we carried on using Latin and Greek to name scientific discoveries. Geography comes from Greek, and dynamo and electrical, even though the ancient Greeks didn't have electric light.

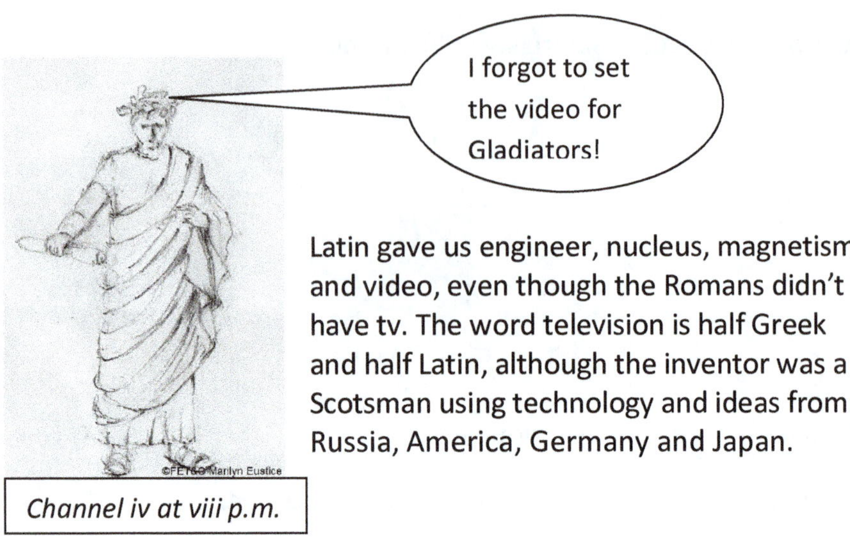

Channel iv at viii p.m.

Latin gave us engineer, nucleus, magnetism and video, even though the Romans didn't have tv. The word television is half Greek and half Latin, although the inventor was a Scotsman using technology and ideas from Russia, America, Germany and Japan.

And it carries on changing.

As a result of all these exciting new discoveries, and our complicated history, the English language has about 490,000 ordinary words. There are also 300,000 technical terms, from science and engineering. If we add them together, everyone in Luton could have more than four words each without ever duplicating. Mostly, we don't use them all. Most people only use about 5000 words in speaking and about 10,000 in writing. But the words we do use might come from any country in the world, even though we call them English, and every year we throw away some old ones and find some new ones, often from other languages, from people with good ideas we want to use.

The American language was originally English, from settlers who went over in the 1600s. In those days, people said yea instead if yes. English in the UK lost that word and all started to say yes. Americans kept it but in modern times it sounds like yeah. Then English people started watching American films and talking like the cowboys and gangsters they saw in them. So they started saying yeah, thinking it was a modern word, when it was only their old word coming home again.

4) Another way words get into English is by something being named after its maker. These words are called eponyms. What do you think was named after Mr Volta? Mr Geiger? Mr, Bunsen? Use a dictionary to look up cardigan, raglan, sandwich, fuchsia and nicotine and find the names of the people they were named after. What did Amelia Bloomer invent?

Questions

1) What language gave us the word video?

2) Explain how Strathclyde got its name.

3) Explain how Wednesday came to have that name.

4) What is French for teeth?

Another way words get into English is by something being named after its maker. These words are called eponyms. What do you think was named after Mr Geiger? Can you find out who invented cardigans and sandwiches.

What time is vii pm?

What does p.m. stand for?

What does it mean to be 'correct'?

When you hear people speak about 'right' or 'wrong' English, what could it mean? Being wrong might involve:

Making no sense at all.

Shoes singing planes she plaster

Those are English words but put together in such a way they seem to have no meaning. If you make sentences carelessly, they can seem to have no meaning for the reader even if they make sense to you. If you make your notes too quickly, they may not make sense to you in a week or two.

Confusing.

Even if there is some sense, you might leave room for more than one meaning.

Running down the road, I saw Mary fall over.

Was Mary running or were you? You have to take a break after you write something. Read it again later and see what it might look like to another person.

Inefficient.

It might be obvious what you mean eventually but it takes too long to get there.

Please can you send us, if you would be so kind, one of those printers which we had last year that worked very well, which I think you called a Lepsark X205 only this time we would like it delivered to our head office at 55 New Rd and make it addressed to Mr. Shandy.

You could grow old waiting for the end of that sentence. Try

Please deliver a new Lepsark X205 printer to Mr. Shandy at 55 New Rd.

Against the rules (and maybe confusing too)

There are also rules about spelling and punctuation that are supposed to make things more clear. If you wrote 'sizzers' I could guess you meant scissors. If you asked me for a wait I might not know you wanted a weight.

He is coming tonight, with Mary, who is going to sing.

does not mean the same as

He is coming tonight with Mary. Who is going to sing?

If you don't know the rules you might confuse the reader.

You may remember from L1 the problem of using the wrong register – being too formal or informal.

There are also rules about what kinds of words are 'correct' and how they should be pronounced. Most people already know that 'correct' English means you ain't supposed to say fings like nuffing or nowt. Gaffer and spuds ain't proper English. File (L5) on dialect explains how these rules came about.

Ugly or irritating

> It has got sense, but it hasn't got like a sound what
> people like, innit?

Different people have different tastes, so what sounds 'pleasing' will vary, but try to remember what it sounds like. If you want to impress someone or get them to do something for you then try to work out what the reader would like to 'hear'. If it is always a matter of taste, whose taste counts most, when and why?

You may find it useful to read the next section on dialect.

What is a dialect and what is 'proper' English?

You already know that English was made up from lots of other languages (L12). It ended up as one language when everybody settled down and all shared their words to make one large collection with the same rules. But it didn't happen in just one day. It took hundreds of years before we all spoke more-or-less the same language. At first, everybody spoke their own version.

Different tribes of people had settled in different areas. For example, the north had lots of Danish words, but the south had more Saxon words. Different areas, with different groups, spoke a different kind of English, with lots of different words and accents.

What some people called a potato, or a spud, the Cornish might call a tatty. One group might say they are getting 'behind' but in Norfolk they would say 'ahind', and they called ladybirds 'Bishey barney bees'.

Different areas had different accents, and you can still tell the difference between people from Liverpool, Glasgow, Newcastle or Cardiff. They have their own sound, and often their own special words.

This became very confusing so, after a while, it was decided to have only one kind of English for writing letters or doing important business. Otherwise, when people travelled about or wrote to someone in another area, they wouldn't understand each other. The kind of English that was chosen was the kind they spoke in the houses of the rich merchants in the south east of the country.

When they invented schools who went to school had to learn that one kind of English. The official kind for reading and writing is called Standard English (SE for short) and the official way to pronounce it is called Received Pronunciation (RP for short).

Having one kind of English for everybody to read and write didn't stop people making up their own words for things and speaking in their own accents. People might use SE to write in school then speak something else at home. There are still big differences in different parts of the country. We still keep adding new words and sounds.

As we gained access to television and films from other countries, and then to the internet, we got to hear how people spoke in other places, and if we liked their music or their clothes then sometimes we borrowed their words and even their accents. People from the UK started to sound as if they had learned English from Australian soaps, American gangster movies or Jamaican sound tracks rather than their parents a neighbours.

Questions for discussion

Do you have any words that are only used in your town, or your family, which wouldn't be understood by outsiders? For example, does anyone at home use special terms for insects or animals or certain kinds of food or geographical features? You can google dialects easily to listen to examples - is there an old dialect in your area and can you understand it? Would it be 'acceptable'?

Do you have words that are used by your age group that local people of other generations don't understand? Where did those words come from?

Tools of the trade

There are lots of easy ways to find out basic facts either from books or the internet. You don't have to remember everything if you know where to look.

Dictionary

There are lots of different kinds. Always use a modern English edition, never American – their spellings are different and so are some of their meanings. We have centre and they have center. Their vest is a waistcoat. Our expression 'keep your pecker up' would sound very rude to them. Most computers have dictionaries attached, and there are lots on line – just google 'dictionary'.

An etymological dictionary will tell you where words came from. If yours is not that kind, you can also try search engines like *http://www.etymonline.com/*.

You can also get specialists dictionaries, for technical terms in certain subjects. Or you could make your own online as you go along. You can get medical dictionaries (or look at *http://www.nhsdirect.nhs.uk)*.

Dictionaries also tell you how to pronounce a word. How do you pronounce aeon (a very long period of time)? The dictionary might spell it out for you as *eon*. This is 'phonetic' spelling. Different dictionaries use different systems. Chambers 20th Century has a simple system.

Think about the different ways of pronouncing refuse, invalid, desert, wound, produce, present, object, row, close, wind and tear.

You will need to know where to place the stress in a word. Some dictionaries will tell you. You could pronounce refuse as rifuz or refus (meaning 'say no' or 'rubbish'). To say no you want to stress the end, or second syllable. To refer to rubbish you need to stress the first syllable. The little mark like an apostrophe – ' - shows that stress comes just before it – refiz' and re'fus.

Thesaurus

You don't need one, but you need to know how to use one, either as a book or online. They offer many different options when you are stuck for a word. You start with one word, perhaps 'large'. You want a better word. Look up the word you know in the back and it will ask you to be more exact. There are three different entries you could try. Each one leads you to a list of alternatives.
> Great (32) has words like main, major, man-size, bulky.
> Extensive (183) has words like spacious, vast, broad, deep
> Large (195) has words like whale, elephant, enormous, gigantic.

They usually give you paragraph numbers not page numbers

You have to be careful. Some of the words are so out of date that nobody will know what you mean. They don't all mean the same thing. You have to explore and choose something that is closer to the exact meaning you wanted.

You can find a thesaurus online (just google for them).

There are plenty of **rhyming dictionaries** (e.g. in Penguin by Rosalind Fergusson, 1985) and many are on line.

*Everyman's **Dictionary of Dates*** does what it says on the cover, with often useless but interesting lists or popes and monarchs. Pears Cyclopaedia has a timeline section with events, showing what happened on the week you were born.

You can get all kinds of dictionaries on line, including dictionaries of music and mythology. Just remember that not everything you read on the internet is true. If it is important you might have to check it in the library too.

Basic terms of grammar

You may not be able to call it to mind at once, but you probably already know quite a lot of what is in this file. You probably heard it at school once and then forgot about it. We are going to need some basic terms to discuss ideas in the next files. We need to talk about certain kinds of words, what they are and how they work. What is the difference, for example, between practice and practise or license and licence? How can the difference be explained?

Nouns are things

table, chair, beetroot, mountain

They may be **concrete** because they are physical

stone, brick, beetroot

or **abstract** because they cannot be seen in themselves, only through other things or other people

love, hate, fear, loyalty, pride

They may be **proper nouns**, which means names

Brighton, Mildred, Henry

or **pronouns** in place of the name

he, she, it, they.

All nouns can be have a describing word, which we call an

adjective. For example, a table can be

red, heavy, expensive, stolen

So could Mildred.

Or a beetroot.

Verbs are 'doing words'. You could

run, jump, shout, sleep or dance

A simple action could happen in the present

he runs

the past

he ran

or the future

he will run.

Sometimes, two verbs work together

he **is running** (for the home team. in 3rd place, out of excuses)

All verbs start with an **infinitive** form and are then changed according to person or tense.

To be (infinitive)

I am   you are   he/she/it is

to see (=infinitive)

I see   you see   he or she or it sees

I am seeing   I shall see   I saw   I would have seen etc. etc.

Verbs can also be qualified, this time by **adverbs.** She may run quickly or slowly. I may shout loudly or whisper quietly.

It is not the word which counts but how it is used.

In cricket you can score something. The thing you score is a run. That is a thing, or a noun. <u>To</u> run is a verb. <u>To</u> whisper is a verb. I can hear <u>a</u> whisper (= noun).

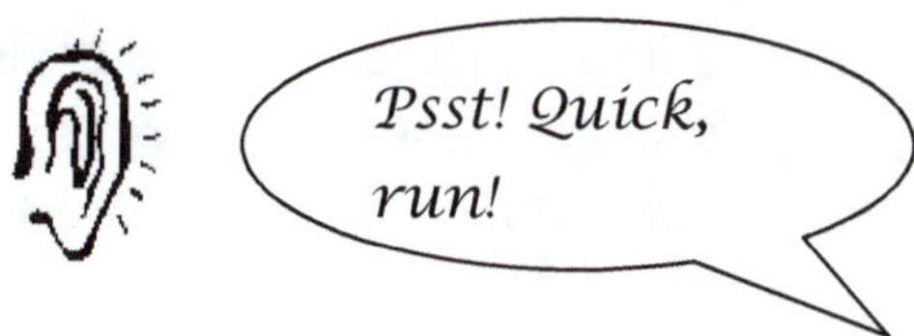

Underline the nouns in these sentences:

Brighton is a dirty old town which Sally only visits reluctantly and on special occasions. She tends to come down once a week, usually for two days, and leaves a sadder but a wiser women. She is sitting there now, sadly wishing it would stop raining.

Now underline the adjectives

Brighton is a dirty old town which Sally only visits reluctantly and on special occasions. She tends to come down once a week, usually for two days, and leaves a sadder but a wiser women. She is sitting there now, sadly wishing it would stop raining.

Now the verbs:

Brighton is a dirty old town which Sally only visits reluctantly and on special occasions. She tends to come down once a week, usually for two days, and leaves a sadder but a wiser women. She is sitting there now, sadly wishing it would stop raining.

And finally the adverbs:

Brighton is a dirty old town which Sally only visits reluctantly and on special occasions. She tends to come down once a week, usually for two days, and leaves a sadder but a wiser women. She is sitting there now, sadly wishing it would stop raining.

Take a break for some silly stuff - collective nouns

> a flock of sheep, a shoal of fish, a fleet of ships or taxis, a sheaf of papers, a swarm of locusts, a batch of cakes, a hand of bananas, gang of navvies, a pride of lions, a pack of wolves

You can find more on various web sites (google 'collective nouns' using UK sites only). Many of them will look as if they have been made up recently, and some of them probably have. That is a problem with the internet. But you can also make up your own for creative use. A flood of plumbers? A bench of football managers? A whisper of librarians? In town, you might need a stew of sheep, or a portion of duck.

Now back to the more serious stuff - agreement of subject and verb

A common basic error in English is to have a lack of agreement between subject and verb

they is coming

or to use a non-standard form in tenses

I seen it done

preposition

A preposition relates one thing to another (to, with, from, at, for.) You can agree **with** a person, **to** a proposal. You can be impatient **with** a person, **at** a situation. Prepositions are not supposed to come at the end of a sentence, but this is a habit up with which we sometimes have to put.

And that is enough to get you through all the other sections. You can come back to this one if you need to. Did you remember some of it from previous years?

What is a sentence?

Stage 1

This is a sentence. This is another sentence. Both of them are short. Both of them are easy to read. You are now on sentence number five. To begin with, keep your sentences as short as you can.

This is a sentence which is going to be difficult to read because it is quite long and the bit you are reading now has to be remembered while you go and read this bit and then you have to read this bit as well before you get any kind of a rest that kind of thing can be very tiring and the reader can find it very irritating and confusing that is why **short sentences are much better.**

If you don't like reading sentences like that, don't write them.

Stage 2

A sentence needs two things – an action and someone to do it.

Harry shouted.

The car swerved.

You will remember that the action words are called verbs:

to shout

to swerve

They can come in various forms, for past or future actions

Harry was shouting.

Harry will be shouting.

Harry would have shouted, but they warned him the baby was asleep.

What matters is that a person (Harry) or a thing (car) has an action (shout, swerve). The action is the verb and the person or thing doing it is the subject.

subject	verb
Harry	shouted
The car	swerved
The student	understood

You can't have a sentence with only a verb

(Who?)   sang

or only a subject

Anna   (did what?)

and you can't put a full stop between the subject and the verb

Anna. Was confused by that full stop.

The full stop should only be used after the subject and the verb have both been written in the same sentence.

Anna was confused by that full stop.

Stage 3

Sometimes the verb needs to be done **to** something or someone. That is the object

subject	verb	object
John	gave	money to charity
The noise	surprised	the audience
The writer	corrected	her mistakes

In real life, sentences are rarely this simple. They often have more than one person or thing and several actions. For example:

> Anna called for Harry and rang the bell twice, but Harry had already left and was sitting on the bus, wondering why she hadn't come round.

The sentence starts with a subject, verb and object (Anna called) but then has lots of other subjects and verbs as well:

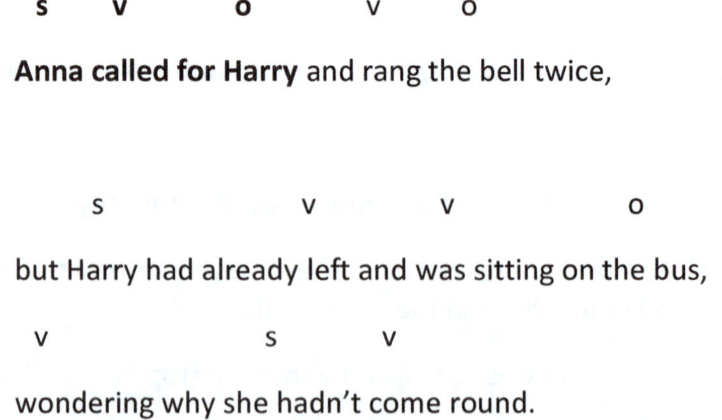

In that example, you have a **main subject** of the sentence and a **main verb** for that subject (Anna, called). Then you have lots of other verbs (rang, left, sitting, wondering) with their own subjects (he, she). Too many verbs can become confusing, especially if it is not very clear what verb belongs to which subject or object:

> Anna sold her car, which was rusty, and Harry warned her the buyer might come back and be angry, but he didn't come round yesterday.

Who is the subject of the verb come round? Harry or the buyer? With short sentences you don't get that kind of confusion. Later, you can join them together with conjunctions.

Conjunctions

Once you have a supply of decent short sentences , you can join them together.

> This example is typed. This example can be printed.

> This example is typed and can be printed.

The word placed at the junction of the two is called a conjunction. In this case it is the most common conjunction (and). Other conjunctions include:

> but, because, which, who, that, therefore, both, either/neither with or/nor, so

For example,

> I was going to visit my aunt. I heard she was in a terrible mood. I changed my mind.

can become

> I was going to visit my aunt but I heard she was in a terrible mood so I changed my mind.

or

> I was going to visit my aunt but I changed my mind because I heard she was in a terrible mood.

It can be very boring to read the same conjunctions used too many times:

> I told him I was going out **but** he said he wanted to stay in

but I said I preferred going out **but** he said we couldn't afford it **but** I told him we could **but** he said we couldn't.

You could (a) try to find another conjunction (b) put the facts in another order (c) just stick to short sentences.

> I told him I was going out but he said he wanted to stay in. When I said I preferred going out he said we couldn't afford it. I thought we could so we argued.

> I wanted to go out but he didn't. I thought we could afford to go but he disagreed.

There are certain **common errors** to watch out for.

1) Starting a sentence with **and or but.** This is sometimes OK in a novel or a newspaper, where it makes dramatic effect.

> I started to climb the dark, creaky stairs. He had promised to meet me. He said nothing would keep him away. But he wasn't there.

> The factory closed today and everybody lost their job. The new manager had promised to bring in new orders. He was paid a large salary to do this. He took many to dinner at the firm's expense. But no orders came in.

It becomes a problem if you do it all the time, especially if you do it by accident:

> I think I know where to use a full stop. But I'm not sure. I asked my tutor about it. And he gave me this sheet.

2) **This, it, she and they** are often used incorrectly.

or

>I went to see my aunt, she is old, she is confused.

>My aunt has a large cat, it pees on the carpet.

These are really separate sentences:

>I went to see my aunt. She is old. She is confused.

>My aunt has a large cat. It pees on the carpet.

To join them together, they need conjunctions:

>I went to see my aunt, who is old and confused.

>My aunt has a large cat which pees on the carpet.

You can't just bung short sentences together with a comma, so use conjunctions to do it properly. (Commas are dealt with in L10)

3) Starting with **'so'** can be a problem. This is OK:

>So many people came we had to close the gates.

But this is not:

>I felt sorry for her. So I went to see her and took some flowers. So she let me in. So I put the kettle on.

Here, 'so' is a conjunction and it would be better as:

>I felt sorry for her so I went to see her. She let me in and I put the kettle on.

or

> I went to see her because I felt sorry for her. When she let me in, I put the kettle on.

Exercises

Take the list of facts and join them together in sentences. Use any conjunctions you wish. How many different ways could you do this?

> The holiday was booked on 5th. The airport was closed. It was foggy. The hotel had to be paid for. We spent two nights in the airport. We had to pay for our food. The airline promised to pay for our food. They did not come back to give us any money or food. When we got to the hotel we wrote to the airline. They said they could not send us a refund. The weather was not their fault.

The following examples all show typical mistakes. Working in groups or pairs if you can, correct them and explain any changes you make. There may be lots of different ways for you to rewrite them.

> There are four jobs free in this office. And twenty five people want to join.

> There are more people than places, this means we have to turn someone down.

> John turned up late. And he forgot to bring his c.v. So we will cross him off the list.

Commas

Some people have been told that commas are to give you a pause for breath. If that were the only rule, heavy smokers would use more commas than athletes. There are better reasons to add them. You don't put commas in just because you want a breath, but you might sometimes take a breath when you find a comma.

There are three main reasons

1) After an introductory word or phrase.

> **Sadly,** Zoe lost her voice

> **Fortunately,** she recovered it.

> **To be honest,** I have never actually tried it

You might use it after starting with Obviously, Finally, Unfortunately.

2) Around information which has been added to an existing sentence.

> They were going to climb Ben Nevis and, if they **enjoyed it,** move on to Everest.

> Arthur, **who is 85**, seems to taking a great interest in three women.

3) Before a conjunction, when two short sentences have been joined to make one more complex example.

> Tracey gave up work seven years ago, but was bored so she started again part-time.

> Samantha used to write one essay a month and consider this hard work**, which** it clearly was not.

You may not wish to bother with the comma if you join two very short sentences, especially if you use 'and':

> This is a short statement and this is another one.

But you may need one for longer examples:

> He was warned not to do it time and time again, **but** he did it anyway

Common mistakes include putting a comma after the conjunction instead of before:

> This is almost right but, not quite.

Or using commas where you need a new sentence:

> This is one sentence, this is another.

should be

> This is one sentence. This is another

or

> This is one sentence and this is another.

You can also use commas

(a) to separate items on a list:

> The colours were red, blue, green and orange.

Note the last two words have 'and' instead of a comma.

(b) To separate narrative from speech:

"Like this," he said.

Exercises:

Add commas, **if appropriate,** to these examples:

Fortunately most people should do very well here.

Jason who was not used to ferries was very ill on the way to France.

Jody noticed that Jason's bag which had been with him in Dover was not on the coach to Paris.

It is not difficult to finish this exercise but you have to concentrate

Nobody knew what was in the dinner but it had food that was red, white, blue, green and brown

"I want to go home" said Jason

Apostrophes

Apostrophes are used for one of two reasons:

1) abbreviation

you're, haven't, can't, shouldn't

These short forms are not often used in formal writing.

2) ownership (usually called possession)

This is where many people get confused. If somebody owns something, the apostrophe is attached to the **owner:**

Becci's problem

You add an apostrophe and an s after the owner. It could be reversed to say:

The problem of Becci

If the owner word already ends in s (two girls), you will make something which is difficult to say

two girls's careers
the career of two girls

so you need to leave out the final s

two girls' careers

If the owner word is a plural that does not end in s (women), the problem does not arise

two women's careers
the careers of two women

two people's jobs
the jobs of two people

Examples:

owner	owned	reversal
Sandra's	essay	the essay of Sandra
The man's	problem	the problem of the man
the day's	work	the work of the day
the men's	room	the room of the men
the lady's	room	the room of the lady
the ladies'	room	the room of the ladies
the dog's	lead	the lead of the dog
The husband's	side	the side of the husband
the cat's	dinner	the dinner of the cat
the cats'	dinners	the dinners of the cats
the student's	list	the list of the student

As with any rule, there are a few annoying exceptions.

We can abbreviate 'it is' to it's. If we then say 'the team lost its number one slot' we cannot write 'it's number one slot' as it would look like 'it is'. Just leave out the apostrophe.

Its new position is bottom of the league and **it's** a shame.

A common confusion takes place in shop signs – what is known as the grocer's apostrophe. If you shorten *cucumbers* to *cucs* then you might write it as *cuc's* because it is an abbreviation. You would **not** write a sign advertising 'fresh cucumber's'.

Exercise:

Add what is necessary, **if** it is necessary, in the right place:

owner	what they own
Alison	bad habits
Carey	guilty secret
the dog	basket
the children	toys
the men	room
the women	group
Celia	millions
Nicola	hobby
Dominic	mind
three boys	nasty habits

Ayesha doesnt feel so confused now shes read this section.

The cat lost its leg

Its five o'clock

Spelling – wot a weerd langwidge

English is a nasty language for spelling. It has a complicated history, which we explore above. Latin, German, French, Greek, Hebrew and Arabic all have different rules for spelling. As English is a mixture of all these languages and several others too, it is not surprising if our own rules don't really work. It is very hard to learn to spell just by learning the rules because:

there are too many of them

there are too many exceptions

it is very boring

Spellcheck is an obvious tool if you are at a computer, but be careful to set it up as UK not US. Even then, it won't know if you write there instead of their. It is worth looking at a few rules and examples that help sometimes. Then we can look at other ways to learn.

ie/ei

i before e – believe, piece, pier, priest

except after c - receive, receipt, deceive

except for weird, seize, weir.

single and double letters (l,t,p,m.)

Careful has one l but carefully has two.

Usual → usually. Travel → travelled. Metal → metallic.

Permit → permitted. Regret → regrettable.

Writing → written

You don't always double the last letter when word gets longer but you probably do, so check the dictionary in case.

ery/ary

Stationery for envelopes and stationary for standing still.

-se/-ce

To advise is a verb and some advice is a noun. To practise and to license but some practice and a licence. Pubs have been licensed (verb) to sell beers and spirits.

able/ible

> desirable, believable, usable, reliable, sociable, irritable

> digestible, suggestible, legible, responsible, possible

There are rules to explain why some are -ible and some –able but they are so complicated it is easier just to remember that it can be a problem and look them up if you are not sure.

ise/ize

Only two common words end -ize

> prize and capsize.

The rest are -ise:

supervise, disguise, surmise, advertise, exercise.

Some words use to have –ize in previous times but the modern forms is now -ise. Some American words spelling still use –ize because they emigrated from the UK a long time ago. They may say organize but we say orgnaise.

Plurals

Words which end in y usually become ies

City = cities duty = duties ally = allies

Words which end in ey usually become eys

Valley = valleys alley = allies chimney = chimnies

homophones

These sound the same (homo=same, phone=sound) but look different when written. There are many in English and certain common mistakes are very dangerous:

To/too/two
there/their/they're
past/passed
course/coarse,
whether/weather
your/you're
its/it's
hear/here

Note also metre/meter, principle/principal, draft/draught, cue/queue, oral/aural, compliment/complement, , sea/see, rein/rain/reign, fate/fete council/counsel, sight/cite/site, berth/birth, right/write/wright as in playwright/rite).

Some words only sound the same if you pronounce them incorrectly.

Could have	is often written incorrectly	could of
Has		as
Caught		court
Lose		loose
Choose		chose

So what do you do now?

You can expect to make mistakes. We all do. The trick is not to be a perfect speller but to take the trouble to check. Recognise when a word is likely to be a problem and look it up. On the other hand, some mistakes are more serous and urgent than others. You can't spell wrongly a word that is important to your special subject (enzyme, pallete, angle, yeast). Some words are so basic you have to try to get them right first (e.g. right and write).

Choose from your corrected work six of the the most important or dangerous mistakes (your tutor can hep you choose). Look them up here to see if there is a simple rule to help you. Often, the rule is too complicated to be much use. In that case, make a list of six of the words. Cover them up. Write them out, uncover the list and see if you were correct.

If you have made any mistakes, do it again. Keep doing it until you have spelled all of them correctly twice. Take a break and try again a few days later. Do this until you have covered all the really important errors, then start again. Keep doing that until you have stopped making the mistakes that do the most damage.

The aim is not to know everything, but to care enough to check. That sends a message to the reader that you can be relied on to use the tools available and to keep an eye on the quality of what is sent out.

Also, when you are trying to 'see' a word, try putting it in the top left hand corner of your mind. Put it in the top left hand corner of the room or your desk and see if it helps.

Exercise in homophones

Enter your suggestions in the spaces provided.

To			
Sea			
One			
Bee			
Write			
Rain			
Queue			
Sight			
So			
Stationery			
Past			
Course			
Whether			
Your			
Waste			
Son			
Pair			
Piece			
Metre			
Draft			
There			
Seed			
Fair			
Plane			
Current			
No			

Answers

(if you are looking here before you filled them in then go away)

owner	what they own
Alison's	bad habits
Carey's	guilty secret
the dog's	basket
the children's	toys
the men's	room
the women's	group
Celia's	millions
Nicola's	hobby
Dominic 's	mind
three boys'	nasty habits

Ayesha doesn't feel so confused now she's read this.

The cat lost its leg

It's five o'clock

To	to	two	
Sea	see		
One	won		
Bee	be		
Write	right	wright	rite
Rain	rein	reign	
Queue	cue		
Sight	Site	cite	
So	sew		
Stationery	stationary		
Past	passed		
Course	coarse		
Whether	weather		
Your	you're		
Waste	waist		
Son	sun		
Pair	pear	pare	
Piece	peace		
Metre	meter		
Draft	draught		
There	they're	their	
Seed	cede		
Fair	fare		
Plane	plain		
Current	currant		
No	know		

Companion volumes by the same author from Justifiedtext.co.uk

How to Learn (Advanced) for undergraduates, A Level and Nat Dip students.

978-0-9926088-8-0

Teaching in FE

978-0-9926088-3-5

Managing Teacher in FE

978-0-9926088-4-2

Reading and Thinking (primary)

978-0-9926088-5-9

All available in paperback or Kindle, from Amazon and any good bookstore

www.ingramcontent.com/pod-product-compliance
Lightning Source LLC
Chambersburg PA
CBHW061514050726
47593CB00002B/557